Between the Monster

and the Saint

Also by Richard Holloway

Between the Monster and the Saint

REFLECTIONS ON THE HUMAN CONDITION

RICHARD HOLLOWAY

CANONGATE

Edinburgh · London · New York · Melbourne

First published in Great Britain in 2008 by
Canongate Books Ltd, 14 High Street,
Edinburgh EH1 1TE

1

British Library Cataloguing-in-Publication Data
A catalogue record for this book is available on
request from the British Library

ISBN 978 1 84767 253 7

Typeset by Palimpsest Book Production Limited,
Grangemouth, Stirlingshire

This book is printed on FSC certified paper

Mixed Sources
Product group from well-managed
forests and other controlled sources
www.fsc.org Cert no. TT-COC-002341
© 1996 Forest Stewardship Council
FSC

Printed and bound by Mackays of Chatham plc, Chatham, Kent

www.canongate.net

For Mark

He curls himself up and protects his head
While he is kicked by heavy boots; on fire and running,
He burns with bright flames; a bulldozer sweeps him
   into a claypit.
Her child. Embracing a teddy bear. Conceived in ecstasy.

I haven't yet learned to speak as I should, calmly.

Czeslaw Milosz

Contents

Acknowledgements

I am extremely grateful to Nick Davies for wise advice on the overall shape of this book, and to Katherine Stanton for suggesting some corrections and improvements to the text.

It will be obvious to anyone who reads this book, or glances at the bibliography, that I owe a great deal to many other writers. I am grateful to them all, but I would like, in particular, to mention five women without whose inspiration my book would never have been written: Hannah Arendt, Andrea Dworkin, Pumla Gobodo-Madikizela, Gitta Sereny, Simone Weil and Virginia Woolf.

Where I have quoted from the Bible I have used the King James version.

Richard Holloway
Edinburgh 2008

Introduction

When I was nine I had a job as a message boy for a grocer's shop at the top of our street. It was a big store with a workforce of eight, both women and men. One morning when the shop was quiet an incident occurred which has stayed in my memory. There was a big store room at the back of the shop, with a long table in the middle, used for measuring and bagging, slicing and sorting. On the morning in question there was a conspiratorial buzz among the male members of the staff, who were all drifting towards the store room. I joined them, wondering what was up. It was obvious that, whatever was afoot, the ringleader was the oldest man on the staff, a self-important person who seemed to think himself a cut above the rest of us. When we had all gathered he hushed us to silence, and a few seconds later one of the women workers came into the room, presumably to pick up something for a customer. As soon as she entered, the door was closed, then locked, and the men surrounded her. The atmosphere, as I remember it, was jokey rather than menacing, and the woman giggled nervously as though she knew what was coming. Mr Self-Importance gave the signal and the men grabbed the woman and lifted her onto the table on her back. Though she struggled a bit, it seemed to me to be more of a lark than a lynching, and she didn't call out for help. I didn't exactly know what was going on, but I played a significant part in what happened. Though she was being held down on her back on the table, her legs were still hanging over the side. Entering the fun, I took hold of her ankles and lifted her legs onto the table, provoking the congratulations of Mr Self-Importance for my assistance. He then shoved his hand under her skirt and groped her. And it was all over. They let her up, she adjusted her clothes, collected whatever it was she had come for, left the room and the men all went back to work. Nothing was said after the incident, and no reference was ever made to it. I stopped working there soon afterwards. Sometimes I would bump into Mr Self-Importance in the town, out with his family, and I used to wonder what went on in his mind about the incident. I also wondered what had got into me, why I did what I did, where it came from, what it was that took over in the store room in that long-gone grocer's shop in Mitchell Street, Alexandria.

I was an introspective little boy who lived mainly in the dreams and dreads of my imagination, prompted by my addiction to reading and movie-going. The fictions I was immersed in on page and screen all communicated a sense of the world as a dangerous and unpredictable place. There seemed to be three main characters abroad on the earth, and though the stories I devoured and the movies I watched played with them in different ways, there appeared to be a single story with variants, endlessly repeated. Sometimes it was obvious good-ness threatened by obvious evil, but that was never a particularly compelling story. In their different ways, the really evil and the truly good seemed to be pretty invulnerable to spiritual attack, which was why it was difficult to make them interesting, probably because they were already so defined and clear about themselves. The really interesting story was about those who were caught between the two invulnerabilities. This plot took many forms, but a favourite from the Hollywood movies of the time was the kid from a tough neighbourhood who was pulled between the craggy priest fighting to save him from a life of crime and the charismatic gang leader out to recruit him for the Mob. The stories and movies I preferred were like that. The real drama lay in the struggle of the character who was tugged between the monster and the saint. Already I could sense that the bad–good man or the good–bad man were more interesting than the definitely good or the certainly bad – probably because I knew intuitively that this was where life would place me. The troubling thing about that assault in the grocer's shop was that it had thrilled as well as appalled me, and had sent a premonitory shiver down my spine.

A few years later I began to immerse myself in one of the most intense descriptions of the human struggle our imagination has contrived: the redemption myth of Christianity. In this drama the moral extremity of the main protagonists is made absolute, as is the fate of the compromised character pulled between them. Perfect and eternal goodness battles with utter and determined evil for the soul of humanity. And sex is one of the battlegrounds. In that light, the incident in the grocer's

shop was a skirmish in a larger war. You do not have to
believe in the truth of the doctrine to acknowledge
that, like a great work of art, the Christian story captures
the reality of our experience. Indeed, it could be
argued that it was developed over the centuries precisely
to account for the human condition. Nowadays we are
more likely to argue over competing versions of the
scientific exposition of human nature than over theological explanations, but the facts we are dealing with
remain the same: our own experience of the mysterious complexity of being human. It is no accident that
from the beginning of recorded history our fictions have
been about our struggles with sex and violence, cruelty
and greed, belonging and loss. These are still the themes
of the films that crowd out the multiplexes and the
books that race up the bestseller lists. Art – in which I
include religion because, whatever else it is, it is certainly
a work of the human imagination – holds a mirror
before humanity, and what we see there should trouble
us profoundly.

In the redemption song of Christianity the preacher
always began by holding that same mirror up to
humanity: this is who you are, he would proclaim; look
at yourselves being pulled between your lower and your
higher impulses, tugged between the monster and the
saint. The old preachers avidly described the temporal
consequences of our actions – relationships broken, lives
destroyed, civilisations corrupted. They also stoked the
fires of hell to scare us into repentance: if common sense
couldn't get us to change our ways, then fear might. It
was at the moment of complete abjection, when we had

recognised the truth about ourselves, that the redemption offer was made: amend your ways, turn from evil
to good, from darkness to light, and God will save you.
There have been many secular variants of that ancient
song. The most dramatic in recent history was the British
Government's campaign in the early days of the AIDS
pandemic to alert vulnerable groups to the dangers of
unprotected sex. The most striking version around today
comes from the green movement, which warns us that
our greedy indifference to the health of the planet is
destroying our own habitat. For many it is already too
late to mend our ways: judgement is coming upon us
like a rising sea and a raging fire. It is the ancient song
embroidered with new themes, the old story embel-
lished with new characters; but the tragic figure at the
centre remains the same: Adam, humanity, *us*.

This book is my version of that old redemption song
– minus the expectation of supernatural rescue: if we can't
redeem ourselves, then no one else is going to do it for
us. I, too, am holding up a mirror for us to look into,
and I am well aware of the ugliness that is reflected there.
But ancient as well as modern wisdom acknowledges that
if men and women are to change their ways they have
to own the reality of their condition: as we say today, they
must no longer be 'in denial'. This is a book about the
human condition, so it is about a paradoxical being: a
moral animal, an evolved creature which has become an
object of interest to itself, a living bundle of drives and
needs that is yet capable of reflection and pity.

The book is in three parts, each section a meditation on some aspect of that turbulent complexity. Part I

explores the ugly fact of human cruelty and the reality of evil. What is it about the human animal that turns it so hideously against its own kind? In wrestling with that question, I look at some heart-stopping examples of human cruelty, such as the practice of systematic torture. The daunting thing here is that torture has made a sophisticated reappearance in our own day. But we are not only cruel to each other, we are monstrously cruel to the other creatures with whom we share the planet. The insidious thing about cruelty to animals, especially those upon whom we depend for food, is that, though it is done to keep our supermarkets stocked with cheap food, it is largely hidden from us. No wonder some poets think the environmental crisis is the way the earth is purging itself of the humans who have so brutally distorted its rhythms and destroyed its balances.

Part II tries to figure out why humans are uniquely prone to this kind of unbalanced sadism and greed. Is it because our big brain is both a blessing and a curse? A blessing, because it has produced the extraordinary richness of human culture; a curse, because it has persuaded us of our uniqueness. In the face of death, our advanced consciousness finds it hard to believe in our own finitude and transience; with the consequence that we have accorded ourselves the status of masters of the whole created order. Nevertheless, we are uncertain about who we are, where we came from and where we are going: and it is from those uncertainties that our religious and intellectual responses to life have developed.

In Part III a faint but unconquerable note of hope

begins to be heard. While human history is a record of cruelty and folly, it is also one of breathtaking achievement in the way our imagination has represented and interpreted the world to us. Art on its own may not be redemptive, but it has the power to challenge and prompt us to gratitude; and gratitude, like pity, is an antidote to our endemic cruelty. But art is not the only redemptive possibility present in the world. The mystery of evil may be an enduring aspect of the human story; but so is the mystery of goodness: the saint is as strong a character in the human narrative as the monster. Like everything else we have invented, religion has been put to evil uses, to such an extent that certain secular thinkers identify it as the root of all evil. Without softening the valid elements of that accusation, the paradox of religion is that its myths and metaphors also provide us with some of the deepest insights into our own condition. Used modestly and understood properly, religion still has much to offer a humanity that is trying to save itself from itself.

Karl Marx famously observed that the philosophers have only interpreted the world, but the point was to change it. I agree with him about that, but change itself needs interpreting. Marx's name will be for ever associated with an attempt to change the world that became monstrous in its ruthlessness. Schemes for universal redemption, whether religious or political, invariably end in cruelty: to force through their programmes they have to drive against the knotted grain of human nature, and to do that they have to purge themselves of pity. Because cruelty is the human curse, and because it is always amplified by the mob, the three sections of this book gradually build to a single theme that opposes group thinking and acting. I believe not only that we cannot live without pity, but that only pity can save us. Pity may only be weakness to the monster, but it is the only strength of the saint.

I

X FORCE

MONSTER

. . . *evil is, not, as we thought,*
deeds that must be punished, but our lack of faith,
our dishonest mood of denial,
the concupiscence of the oppressor.

W.H. AUDEN

Of the many illuminations of art, an important one is the way it helps us realise that we are not alone in our struggles and confusions: others have been there too, and sometimes it helps to read about what they have been through. My boyhood experience in the back room of that grocer's shop left a stain on my memory. Events from his past prompted a more troubling remembrance in Blake Morrison, recalled in his book *As If*, which explored events surrounding the murder of little James Bulger in 1993. While he was away from home, covering the trial, he had bad dreams, one of which was different from the others:

This isn't waking and remembering something bad from the day before. This is waking and remembering exactly the bad thing, even though it happened a quarter of a century before. Yesterday must have triggered it, and guilt I'd long forgotten. Dust, mice, mothballs, furniture polish, semen, bleach.

The dream takes him back to 1967 when he was fourteen, to a party at Lucy Kerrigan's, whose parents had gone out for the night:

> In the kitchen . . . I see Mick Turner snogging with Lucy, then breaking off to talk to his mate Pat Connolly about Burnley (the football team) as if the kiss hadn't happened or as if it had happened to someone else. Lucy stands there, beatific with a Babycham bottle. She and Mick kiss some more, by the cupboard under the stairs, then he opens the door and draws her inside . . . Mick comes out of the broom cupboard, adjusting his clothes, and nods at Pat, who takes his place . . . Two minutes later, Pat comes out. 'Go on, Blake, get in there,' he says . . . I close the door behind me, and inhale the smell of dust, mice, perfume, mothballs, cider, furniture polish, semen, bleach. Lucy is moaning against the coat-hooks. She stretches her arms out and draws me into her sourapple kiss.[1]

He kisses, fondles, gropes her, but decides not to go all the way. He leaves the cupboard; grabs a drink; someone else takes his place. Later, sick, sore, crying, Lucy tells her friends that seven boys had sex with her in the broom cupboard. There is indignation among her friends, but no charges are ever brought. Except now, twenty-five years later, against Blake Morrison by his own conscience. Where did that teenage gang-bang come from? What got into them? Morrison's memory is of an event that was far more serious than the one I remembered, but that ugly incident in the back room of a shop can be thought of as the first milestone on a road that stretches far into the moral distance; and we know from recent as well as ancient history what the far end of that road looks like. It reaches from furtive groping to the organised and systematic raping of women, as men are taken over by a force that turns their victims into degraded objects.

Since women have been the main victims of this kind of degradation down the ages, it is no surprise that they have thought about it more searchingly than men. In exploring the forces that provoke such behaviour, I want to make use of the writings of five women, beginning with a remarkable essay by Simone Weil on *The Iliad*, which she calls the 'Poem of Force'. Through an investigation of the tragic vision of Homer, Weil says humans are at the mercy of an energy that plays with them the way a cat toys with a mouse. This is how she describes it:

> To define force – it is that X that turns anybody who is subjected to it into a *thing*. Exercised to the limit, it turns man into a thing in the most literal sense: it makes a corpse out of him. Somebody was here, and the next minute there is nobody here at all; this is a spectacle *The Iliad* never wearies of showing us.[2]

I shall try later to say something about the origin of this X, but if we think of it as any compulsion that turns those who are subjected to it into things, then it is obvious that human sexuality is one of its most powerful modes, seen in its most brutally objectifying form in rape. There is no doubt that looking at women as sexual objects is a dominant aspect of male heterosexuality, and there are few men who have not experienced its disturbing power. It is hard to resist the impulse, which is why 'custody of the eyes' is such a strong theme in the attempts of religion to restrain male sexuality; and it is why the covering or uncovering of the female body in public continues to agitate some religious authorities.

One of the most challenging studies of the force of male sexuality is Andrea Dworkin's book *Intercourse*. The epigraph to the book immediately captures the devastating honesty of the approach: 'He lost no time, got his belt undone, said: "I could go through you like butter."'[3] From the epigraph to the last page we are made to confront the implacable force of male sexuality, which Dworkin reduces to its basic essential as 'the fuck'. Significantly, she calls the first part of her book 'Intercourse in a Man-Made World'. She acknowledges that man himself is worried by the way he can be taken over by the force of sex and become the driven victim of his own desires; but she knows that woman has been the primary casualty of a world created partly to express and partly to control the male sexual urge. The system that established male domination was based not only on brute force, but on law and religious authority. Though the intention was to establish the authority of men over women, it was also aimed at preventing men from destroying their own privileges by over-indulgence. Implicit in the structures that define the man-made world is the recognition that the force of sexuality can dominate the dominators and threaten the balance of male control. The men who were party to the sexual molestation of that woman in the back room of a grocer's shop, and the boys who raped Lucy in the cupboard under the stairs in her own home, were all dominators who were themselves dominated by the imperious force of sexuality. It is the oldest story in the book: the man, often a figure of authority in politics or religion, who is brought low because of his inability to control a sudden access of sexual desire which occurs in the wrong place, at the wrong time, with the wrong person.

Dworkin traces variations of this vicious circle throughout her book. One of the book's many riches is the depth of her reading of other texts In Chapter 2, 'Skinless', she explores Kobo Abe's novel, *The Woman in the Dunes*, in which a man lost in sand dunes is trapped with a woman in a deep hole. He is kept prisoner to clear the sand and to have sex with the woman. The sand stands for the suffocating, enveloping quality his need for sex with a woman can have for a man. It also accounts for man's ancient ambivalence towards women, an ambivalence that can turn easily to hatred, which can itself become a perverted source of pleasure, as men use sex to humiliate and degrade women. When this happens, like the impersonal force of nature itself, men act without any sense of human sympathy. Dworkin writes,

> The sand in *The Woman in the Dunes* is life itself with its crushing disregard for personality or fairness or reason or the defences built up against its unceasing and form-less flow: life here is precisely identical with sexuality, also crushing, formless, shapeless, merciless . . . Carried by life and sex towards death, the human experience is one of being pushed until crushed.[4]

The metaphor of engulfing, enfolding sand reaches into our deepest anxieties about the power sex has over us. It is the fragility of our own self-control in the face of the implacable force of nature, as well as our ambivalence towards it, that is most disturbing to us. Part of us wants to surrender to its irresistible force, while something else in us is horrified by its indifference and tries to struggle against it, overcome it, order it.

Where does this X get its power from? Simone Weil offers us a clue in her analysis of violence, the other great force that reduces to a thing those who are subjected to it. Violence is the theme of *The Iliad*. She writes:

> It springs from the subjection of the human spirit to force, that is, in the last analysis, to matter. This subjection is the common lot, although each spirit will bear it differently, in proportion to its own virtue. No one in *The Iliad* is spared by it, as no one on earth is.[5]

The word to note there is *matter*. 'It springs from the subjection of the human spirit to force, that is, in the last analysis, to *matter*.' This is close to Dworkin's sand metaphor: 'the density of the endlessly moving, formless sand: which is life and its inevitable, massive, incomprehensible brutalities; which is sex, with . . . its omnipresent, incorrigible, massive demands'.[6] If we are to gain any useful insight into the human condition, we have to begin by acknowledging that we are all subordinate to the gravitational pull of a universe which is indifferent to the creatures who are subjected to its remorseless drives. We are thrown into an existence, the springs of which we are only just beginning to understand.

Current scientific thinking holds that our universe had a beginning: there was nothing; then, in an instant, there was something. The initiating event is misleadingly called the Big Bang, which suggests an originating explosion, whereas the reality seems to have been an unbelievably rapid expansion, more like blowing up a balloon than setting off a firework. But where did it come from? The human mind is incapable of abandoning the search for causes, and since scientists cannot get behind that originating event, they offer a transitional myth, borrowed from mathematics, to fill the gap. Since there was no 'there' there before the Big Bang, they say that around fourteen billion years ago the universe sprang into existence out of a 'singularity'. Singularities are unknowns that defy the current understanding of physics: infinitely small, infinitely dense somethings from which everything has emerged. We are the far-flung residue of that originating mystery. While we cannot get behind the first breath of the expanding universe, or understand what force began to blow up the balloon, we do know quite a lot about what has happened since. We know that inanimate matter existed for billions of years before the animate emerged, but that at some point life was aroused in non-living matter by the operation upon it of forces we are still quite incapable of imagining. In 1953 Watson and Crick discovered DNA, a molecule that stores vast amounts of coded information – our genes – and replicates itself in order to make new cells loaded with the same information and self-replicating capability. This process is the miracle of life. The first gene is thought to have appeared more than three and a half billion years ago in the lifeless saline seas of the young planet earth. Scientists speculate that a combination of powerful natural forces,

such as sunlight, geothermal heat, radioactivity and light-
ning, provided the critical jolts of energy that made the
chemical reactions possible. However we account for it,
the seismic energy of that force still drives through us,
as it drives through all earth's life forms, and it is imperi-
ously indifferent to us and our values.

> The force that through the green fuse drives the flower
> Drives my green age; that blasts the roots of trees
> Is my destroyer.[7]

Schopenhauer went so far as to say nature waged war
on humans, because it knew no morality except its own
will to live and replicate itself.[8] It is at its most tyran-
nical in the reproductive drive, sex, where it can quench
not only normal human sympathy, but rationality as
well. But we probably see it at its most terrifying in
battle. Here is Simone Weil again:

> Battles are fought and decided by men . . . who have
> undergone a transformation, who have dropped either to
> the level of inert matter, which is pure passivity, or
> to the level of blind force, which is pure momentum
> . . . however caused, this petrifactive quality of force,
> twofold always, is essential to its nature . . . Its power
> of converting a man into a thing is a double one, and
> in its application double-edged. To the same degree,
> though in different fashions, those who use it and those
> who endure it are turned to stone.[9]

It is in the context of these remorseless energies that
humanity has struggled to find space for order and kindness in its life. Inhibited by its highly evolved brain from

living an unselfconscious life entirely dominated by
instinct, humanity had to hammer out a painful compromise with itself, whereby it traded the full blaze of
instinctive expression for the gentle warmth of social
good. This compromise is usually described as 'civilisa-
tion', and it is always precarious, because the uneasy
bargain on which it is based is not one that all are able
to make. The shorthand term for those who refuse the
compromises of human sympathy is 'evil', which has
been defined as humanity turning against itself.[10]

There are two fundamental theories about the origin
of evil. The situational perspective claims that individuals turn against society because of early childhood
experiences of violence that shamed and degraded them.
Children who have absorbed trauma in their early years
have to shut down emotionally to protect themselves.
The move from victim to aggressor gives them back
the self-respect they lost in their childhood, while their
emotional frigidity anaesthetises them against any
sympathy they might feel for their targets. In his study
of violence J. Gilligan writes:

> The prison inmates I work with have told me repeat-
> edly, when I asked them why they had assaulted someone,
> that it was because 'he disrespected me,' or 'he disrespected
> my visit' (meaning 'visitor'). The word disrespect is so
> central in the vocabulary, moral value system, and psycho-
> dynamics of these chronically violent men that they have
> abbreviated it into the slang term, 'he dis'ed me'.[11]

The other perspective on the formation of the evil character maintains that it cannot simply be the consequence

of childhood trauma, since most people who have suffered in childhood do not turn into monsters. People have free will. Those who choose evil are responsible for the choices they make, the paths they take. After all, people can choose *not* to commit evil. The issue is obviously more complex than a straightforward choice between these two theories. While it is true that those who have been traumatised when young are more likely to fall into a pattern of repetition of the aggression they suffered (just as those who have been loved are more likely to love others in later life), how individuals turn out depends on a number of unpredictable factors. A particularly potent one is whether they have been 'violently coached'; a more hopeful one is whether they were exposed to good experiences that annulled the humiliation they suffered and helped to restore their sense of identity. Those who turn out to be aggressors are likely to have had direct or indirect encouragement to be violent.

In her book, *A Human Being Died that Night*, Pumla Gobodo-Madikizela describes her troubled reactions to the hours she spent interviewing Eugene de Kock, the chief Government assassin during South Africa's apartheid era. Labelled 'Prime Evil' by the media, de Kock was the commander of the Vlakplaas counter-insurgency group which executed dozens of opponents of the apartheid Government. He became prominent during the Truth and Reconciliation Commission, where he gave detailed information about the deaths of anti-apartheid activists. He was sentenced to 212 years in prison for crimes against humanity. Eugene de Kock's childhood was marked by emotional abuse at the hands of a brutal, hard-drinking father, who also mistreated his wife. One way of accounting for de Kock's violent behaviour is to see it as revenge for his early sufferings. However, as with all obsessive behaviour, his constant aggressions failed to relieve the inner needs that drove them. This is an example of what Simone Weil described as the petrifactive quality of force: both those who use it and those who endure it are turned to stone. It is comforting to think of de Kock and people like him as extreme cases, wounded animals ready to strike when the moment comes. What is disconcerting is the discovery that 'good' people with no trauma in their background are also capable of co-operating with and enjoying the spectacle of great cruelty. That is why it is worth noting a fuller definition of evil given by Philip Zimbardo: 'Evil consists in intentionally behaving in ways that harm, abuse, demean, dehumanise, or destroy innocent others – *or using one's authority and systemic power to encourage or permit others to do so on your behalf* [my italics].'[12] Even if we believe in the supremacy of personal responsibility, it is obvious that the social context can easily override the morality of the individual. Zimbardo calls this phenomenon 'situational force', which is another way of saying 'going with the crowd', something most of us have been guilty of, even if it was only in weakly supporting the intolerant prejudices of those to whom we were beholden in some way. Zimbardo writes: 'A large body of evidence in social psychology supports the concept that situational power triumphs over individual power in given contexts.'[13] This means that, while we may not ourselves have the stomach for a life of violence, we can easily become complicit in violence done on our behalf. I shall explore this theme later, but I want to touch now on an even uglier side to humanity's addiction to violence.

It is no accident that critics and commentators frequently link sex and violence together as though they were a single phenomenon, *sexandviolence*. This is more than a recognition that they are both primal forces in nature, including human nature. It is to recognise that they are erotically charged, packed with the possibility of giving pleasure to participant and onlooker, described by Auden as 'the concupiscence of the oppressor'. Nietzsche was the psychologist who explored this gloomy area with the most penetrating insight. *On the Genealogy of Morals* considers where the urge to punish came from.

> To ask it again: to what extent can suffering balance debts or guilt? To the extent that to make suffer was in the highest degree pleasurable, to the extent that the injured party exchanged for the loss he had sustained, including the displeasure caused by the loss, an extra-ordinary counterbalancing pleasure: that of making suffer – a genuine festival . . . To see others suffer does one good, to make others suffer even more: this is a hard saying but an ancient, mighty, human, all-too-human principle . . . Without cruelty there is no festival: thus the longest and most ancient part of human history teaches – and in punishment there is so much that is festive.[14]

The erotic possibilities of the theatre of public cruelty have been exploited by humanity for centuries, right down to the reality TV shows of today. We have been geniuses at crafting set pieces of torture and execution, designed to entertain as well as deter the public. Before they were banned, seats at public executions were as keenly sought after as tickets for violent blockbuster films are in our own day. One of the most celebrated executions in history took place in Paris in 1757, witnessed by a large crowd, some in luxury seats provided for state officials and clergy. We know that Casanova was present, and several times had to turn away his eyes and stop his ears because the spectacle was so ghastly. Robert-François Damiens, a French soldier, had tried to assassinate King Louis XV by stabbing him as he got into his carriage at Versailles. Though his attempt failed, he was found guilty of *lèse-majesté* and parricide. The sentence was execution by a form of torture called the *amende honorable*. History has preserved an eye-witness account of what took place:

On 2 March 1757 Damiens the regicide was condemned 'to make the *amende honorable* before the main door of the Church of Paris', where he was to be 'taken in a cart, wearing nothing but a shirt, holding a torch of burning wax weighing two pounds'; then, 'in the said cart, to the Place de Grève, where, on a scaffold that will be erected there, the flesh will be torn from his breasts, arms, thighs and calves with red hot pincers, his right hand, holding the knife with which he committed the said parricide, burnt with sulphur, and, on those places where the flesh will be torn away, poured molten lead, boiling oil, burning resin, wax and sulphur melted together and then his body drawn and quartered by four horses and his limbs and body consumed by fire, reduced to ashes and his ashes thrown to the winds.'

Bouton, an officer of the watch, left us his account: 'The sulphur was lit, but the flame was so poor that only the top skin of the hand was burnt, and that only slightly. Then the executioner, his sleeves rolled up, took the steel pincers, which had been specially made for the occasion, and which were about a foot and a half long, and pulled first at the calf of the right leg, then at the thigh, and from there at the two fleshy parts of the right arm; then at the breasts. Though a strong, sturdy fellow, this executioner found it so difficult to tear away the pieces of flesh that he set about the same spot two or three times, twisting the pincers as he did so, and what he took away formed at each part a wound about the size of a six-pound crown piece.

'After these tearings with the pincers, Damiens, who cried out profusely, though without swearing, raised his head and looked at himself; the same executioner dipped an iron spoon in the pot containing the boiling potion, which he poured liberally over each wound. Then the ropes that were to be harnessed to the horses were attached with cords to the patient's body; the horses were then harnessed and placed alongside the arms and legs, one at each limb . . . The horses tugged hard, each pulling straight on a limb, each horse held by an executioner. After a quarter of an hour, the same ceremony was repeated and finally, after several attempts, the direction of the horses had to be changed, thus: those at the arms were made to pull towards the head, those at the thighs towards the arms, which broke the arms at the joints. This was repeated several times without success. He raised his head and looked at himself. Two more horses had to be added to those harnessed to the thighs, which made six horses in all. Without success.

'Finally, the executioner, Samson, said to Monsieur Le Breton that there was no way or hope of succeeding, and told him to ask their Lordships if they wished to have the prisoner cut into pieces. Monsieur Le Breton, who had come down from town, ordered that renewed efforts be made, and this was done; but the horses gave up and one of those harnessed to the thighs fell to the ground. The confessors returned and spoke to him again. He said to them (I heard him): "Kiss me, gentlemen." The parish priest of St Paul's did not dare to, so Monsieur de Marsilly slipped under the rope holding the left arm and kissed him on the forehead. The executioners gathered round and Damiens told them not to swear, to carry out their task and that he did not think ill of them; he begged them to pray to God for him, and asked the parish priest in St Paul's to pray for him at his first mass.

'After two or three attempts, the executioner Samson and he who had used the pincers each drew out a knife from his pocket and cut the body at the thighs instead of severing the legs at the joints; the four horses gave a tug and carried off the two thighs after them, namely, that of the right side first, the other following; then the same was done to the arms, the shoulders, the arm-pits and the four limbs; the flesh had to be cut almost to the bone, the horses pulling hard carried off the right arm first and the other one afterwards.

'When the four limbs had been pulled away, the confessors came to speak to him; but his executioner told them that he was dead, though the truth was that I saw the man move, his lower jaw moving from side to side as if he were talking. One of the executioners even said shortly afterwards that when they had lifted the trunk to throw it on the stake, he was still alive. The four limbs were untied from the ropes and thrown on the stake set up in the enclosure in line with the scaffold, then the trunk

and the rest were covered with logs and faggots, and fire
was put to the straw mixed with this wood.

'In accordance with the decree, the whole was
reduced to ashes. The last piece to be found in the
embers was still burning at half-past ten in the evening.
The pieces of flesh and the trunk had taken about four
hours to burn . . . '[15]

Two details in that description break the heart. Writhing
in agony on the scaffold, Damiens asked his confessors
to kiss him. Though the priest of St Paul's refused this
office of mercy, Monsieur de Marsilly slipped under the
rope and kissed him on the forehead. The other devastating detail is when Bouton tells us that Damiens twice
raised his head to look at himself as his body was being
torn asunder. It is hard to think about that look; even
harder to fathom it. Was it a look of disbelief? A look
of farewell? The *amende honorable* was so horrifying it
was outlawed in 1791. But torture never vanished from
the earth, and it has made a dramatic reappearance in
our own day. What is hard to acknowledge is that, in
the right circumstances, most of us are capable of taking
part in it. This was established by the famous obedience
experiment conducted by the social psychologist Stanley
Milgram in 1963, in which people were encouraged to
'electrocute' peers as punishment for a mistake. Milgram
established the experiment because he wanted to understand how so many 'good' Germans became involved in
the murder of millions of Jews.

Rather than search for dispositional tendencies in the
German national character to account for the evil of

this genocide, he believed that features in the situation played a crucial role; that obedience to authority was a 'toxic trigger' for wanton murder. After completing his research, Milgram extended his scientific conclusions to a very dramatic prediction about the insidious and pervasive power of obedience to transform ordinary American citizens into Nazi death camp personnel: 'If a system of death camps were set up in the United States of the sort we had seen in Nazi Germany, one would be able to find sufficient personnel for those camps in any medium-sized American town.'[16]

The history of the US war on terror illustrates the dramatic prescience of Milgram's observation. The approval of torture by the leaders of the United States Government is as well documented as the practice itself. Asked during a radio interview if he was in favour of a 'dunk in the water' for terrorist detainees, Vice President Cheney said he was, declaring that as far as he was concerned the question was 'a no-brainer'.[17] The homely-sounding 'dunk in the water' is actually an ancient and highly effective torture routine called waterboarding. It was used as an interrogation routine during the Italian Inquisition in the 1500s, but its most notorious use in recent history — until the Iraq War — was by the infamous Khmer Rouge regime in Cambodia in the 1970s. In an article on the subject, American journalist Julia Layton described the technique:

> Waterboarding as it is currently described involves strapping a person to an inclined board, with his feet raised and his head lowered. The interrogators bind the person's arms and legs so he can't move at all, and they cover

his face. In some descriptions, the person is gagged, and some sort of cloth covers his nose and mouth; in others, his face is wrapped in cellophane. The interrogator then repeatedly pours water onto the person's face. Depending on the exact setup, the water may or may not actually get into the person's mouth and nose; but the physical experience of being underneath a wave of water seems to be secondary to the psychological experience. The person's mind believes he is drowning, and his gag reflex kicks in as if he were choking on all that water falling on his face.[18]

Torture such as waterboarding by the US has followed a well-established pattern. According to John Gray, American forces were following a well-trodden path here. Torture was used by Russia in Chechnya, by the French in Algeria and by the British in Kenya. But the modern American technique is different to these historic precedents, which mainly inflicted extreme physical pain. In Iraq, as well as in their network of detention centres throughout the world, American interrogators have used psychological pressure, including sexual humiliation, a particularly potent weapon in a Muslim culture. Gray says that by using these techniques the US has imprinted an indelible image of American depravity on the population of Iraq and ensured that no American-backed regime could ever achieve legitimacy.[19]

'Getting Away with Torture' is the chilling title of the Human Rights Watch report on the abuses, tortures and murder of prisoners by US military and civilian personnel since 9/11. While junior members of the military regime at Abu Ghraib prison in Iraq have been tried and convicted – President Bush's seven 'bad apples' in an otherwise immaculate military barrel – none of the architects of the system has been called to justice. This is the conclusion of the report:

> It has become clear that torture and abuse have taken place not solely at Abu Ghraib but rather in dozens of detention facilities worldwide, that in many cases the abuse resulted in death or severe trauma, and that a good number of the victims were civilians with no connection to al-Qaeda or terrorism. There is also evidence of abuse at controlled 'secret locations' abroad and of authorities sending suspects to third-country dungeons around the world where torture was likely to occur. To date, however, the only wrongdoers being brought to justice are those at the bottom of the chain of command. The evidence demands more. Yet a wall of impunity surrounds the architects of the policies responsible for the larger pattern of abuses.[20]

Among the 'architects', Philip Zimbardo names President Bush, Vice President Cheney and Donald Rumsfeld.

The excesses of both sides in the War on Terror, like the excesses of Nazi Germany, reveal how easy it is, when the circumstances are ripe, for obedience to authority to trigger the human, all too human, tendency to unspeakable violence in people with no particular trauma in their background. We might even say that 'good' people who enlist obediently in evil practices are more culpable than those whose childhood trauma predisposed them towards violent aggression. Significantly, obedience to authority is considered a virtue in religion as well as in the military, and both go to great lengths to instil it in their members.

In the case of the military the logic, though unsettling, is obvious. A disciplined army requires soldiers to submerge their individuality for the sake of the group task. The difference between trained soldiers and an undisciplined rabble is that professionals work within a group to achieve an objective and submit themselves to the discipline of a common aim; whereas a mob is an inchoate mass that is as likely to take flight as turn and fight. Nevertheless, obedience to authority has a dark side, and history affords many examples of atrocities committed by men who claimed they were only obeying orders. The habit of obedience, too deeply instilled, can destroy the moral and rational autonomy of the individual; this is a spiritual disease that is prevalent among adherents of certain religions. While obedience may be tactically useful in achieving limited temporal ends, it is stultifying when it becomes a moral and intellectual default position. When that happens it places institutional authority above truth, so that truth is no longer what is the case, but what is asserted by authority to be the case. When Pope Urban VIII condemned Galileo's claim that the sun was immovable in its place and that the earth revolved round it, he pronounced his judgement not on the basis of investigation of the issue but on that of a twofold authority: the Bible and his own office. In the religious context 'truth' too easily becomes what authority says it is. Sometimes this can be endearingly old-fashioned, a simple refusal to accept unwelcome facts; but sometimes it can be the prelude to horror, as the flames that lick round the religious imagination and explode among us today clearly testify. The need to obey, to submit our freedom to the control of absolute authority, may be nostalgia in our DNA for the days when we were driven unresistingly by the force of nature. This may account for its overwhelming attraction, as well as for its formidable power over us. Something in us wants to be pulled away from the responsibilities of the autonomous self back to the state of nature. History is full of examples of whole peoples who abandoned the rigours of freedom for the consolations offered by infallible authority, but none was more terrifying in its consequences than Nazi Germany.

Gitta Sereny wrote a couple of books to show how it was obedience to authority that prompted two very different men to assist in the massacre of millions in Nazi Germany. The first of her Nazi books was about Franz Stangl, who had been Kommandant of Treblinka, one of the four extermination camps in German-occupied Poland. Stangl was sentenced to life imprisonment for co-responsibility in the murder of 900,000 people in Treblinka. Her other book was a study of Albert Speer, the architect of Nazi Germany and Hitler's right-hand man. In the preface to the book about Stangl, *Into that Darkness*, she wrote:

> Over the months of the Nuremberg trials . . . I felt more and more that we needed to find someone capable of explaining to us how presumably normal human beings had been brought to do what he had done . . . an evaluation of such a person's background . . . might teach us to understand better to what extent evil in human beings is created by their genes, and to what extent by their society and environment.[21]

Sereny did not use the language of situational force, but her mention of genes, society and environment is another way of characterising the 'X that turns anybody who is subjected to it into a thing'. Though we never see the X in its own essence, it is revealed to us in the forms it adopts to achieves its ends. One way to characterise it is the accumulated weight of events – from the beginning of the universe to the person we happened to bump into at a party last night – which lie behind the destiny of a single character in the rolling narrative of human history. Most of us are determined and programmed by factors over which we have little control. We may pride ourselves on our autonomy and the ethical power of the choices we have made, but the right circumstances might surprise us by the swiftness with which our integrity would melt in the ecstasy of the mob. Few are immune to this possibility, though, as we shall see, there are always some who are immune to the pressure of the usual determinants and refuse to march to the drumbeat of authority. And they are usually the first to face history's firing squads.

The men Sereny studied, Stangl and Speer, certainly knew how to march in step, and their careers displayed the toxic power of obedience to authority in the context of Nazi Germany. Sereny discovered in their childhoods a similar denial of love to the one experienced by de Kock. Unlike Speer, Stangl was an unremarkable man. Diana Athill worked with Sereny on the book about Stangl, and says this about him in her memoirs:

> I still think – of how that unremarkable man became
> a monster as the result of a chain of choices between
> right and wrong – and the way in which no one he

respected intervened in favour of the right, while a
number of people he respected . . . behaved as though
wrong were right . . . Stangl did not have a strong centre
– had probably been deprived of it by a dreary childhood – so he became a creature of the regime. Other
people without much centre didn't – or not to the
same extent – so some quality inherent in him (perhaps
lack of imagination combined with ambition) must
have been evident to those who picked him for his
appalling jobs. But it was surely environment rather
than genes which made him what he became. [22]

Environment certainly, but the more significant factor,
I think, lies in that tell-tale phrase 'lack of imagination'.
Hannah Arendt made a similar judgement about another
unremarkable man without a strong centre who also
became a monster. Otto Adolf Eichmann, a former Nazi
lieutenant colonel who fled from Germany in 1950,
was kidnapped by the Israeli Secret Service on 11th
May, 1960 and flown to Israel to stand trial. Eichmann
had joined the SS in 1932 and did various jobs for
them. Though he himself never pulled a trigger or
manned a mobile gassing van, he ended up as the logis-
tical wizard who organised the transportation of Jews
to the death camps. In describing him, Arendt coined
the phrase 'the banality of evil' to capture the dreari-
ness and predictability of his personality.

When I speak of the banality of evil, I do so only on
the strictly factual level, pointing to a phenomenon
which stared one in the face at the trial. Eichmann was
not Iago and not Macbeth, and nothing would have
been further from his mind than to determine with

Richard III 'to prove a villain'. Except for an extra-ordinary diligence in looking out for his personal advancement, he had no motives at all. He *merely*, to put the matter colloquially, *never realized what he was doing* . . . He was not stupid. It was sheer thoughtless-ness – something by no means identical with stupidity – that predisposed him to become one of the greatest criminals of that period.[23]

When we turn to Speer the picture is more complex. Like Eichmann, Speer killed no one and felt no enmity, hatred or even dislike for the millions in Eastern Europe, Christians and Jews, who were systematically slaugh-tered. Sereny says he felt *nothing*, because there was a dimension in him that was missing, a capacity to feel that his childhood had blotted out, allowing him to experience not love, but only romanticised substitutes for it. (She says there was a strong erotic bond between Speer and Hitler – never sexualised, but hypnotically present all the same.) Pity and empathy weren't part of Speer's emotional vocabulary. He could feel deeply, but only indirectly – through music or landscape or art. His feelings could also be aroused through what Sereny calls visual hyperbole. He was the begetter of the great Nazi set pieces, such as the Cathedral of Light, with its flags and thousands of men at attention, motionless like pillars, as well as the rows of blond children, eyes shining, arms stiffly raised. This became beauty to him and – another substitute for love – allowed him to *feel*.

But the conclusion of his story is that he did finally learn to feel with real authenticity, and to enter, for the first time, the experience of others. He acknowledged his part in Hitler's madness and came to a horrifying realisation of what had been done. Out of all this emerged a different Speer. In a final paragraph Sereny summed him up:

> This was a very serious man who knew more about that bane of our century, Hitler, than anyone else. This was an erudite and solitary man who, recognizing his deficiencies in human relations, had read five thousand books in prison to try to understand the universe and human beings, an effort he succeeded in with his mind but failed in with his heart. Empathy is finally a gift, and cannot be learned, so, essentially, returning into the world after twenty years (in prison), he remained alone. Unforgiven by so many for having served Hitler, he elected to spend the rest of his life in confrontation with this past, unforgiving of himself for having so nearly loved a monster.[24]

Let me pause before those daunting words: 'Empathy is finally a gift, and cannot be learned,' and compare them to words from Simone Weil:

> He who does not recognise to what extent shifting fortune and necessity hold in subjection every human spirit, cannot regard as fellow-creatures nor love as he loves himself those whom chance separated from him by an abyss. Only he who has measured the dominion of force, and knows how not to respect it, is capable of love and justice.[25]

What can save us from despair at our own emotional incapacity is the fact that we can make a start at change by understanding ourselves. We may lack the innate ability to be empathetic, to identify with the pain of others, but if we succeed in touching our own feelings, reaching our own grief and shame, we can start to practise projective identification with others. In my final chapter I shall try to show how we can measure the way in which force has used us and through us used others; how we can recognise that fortune and necessity hold us all in subjection; and how we can identify with others and refuse ever to turn them into things. This ability to feel ourselves into the lives of others is the root of a morality of sensitivity that refuses to become an unconscious instrument of force.

Apart from our failure to feel the pain we have caused others, another challenge we face is to avoid becoming evil in response to the evil that has been done to us, thereby affording force a double victory. This means we have to think not only about how we may have damaged others, but also about how to respond to those who have damaged us. Any sensible society has to protect itself against the depredations of those who have turned against humanity, whatever theory is held about the factors that produced them. Martin Luther King said that while a law could make no man love him, it could stop him from lynching him. This is why there will always be a defensive need for armed forces, for police, and for a criminal justice system. But, if we care for the values of the society we inhabit, the automatic desire to respond to the force of evil with the evil of force is a reaction worth exploring. If Nietzsche's guess about the origin of punishment is near the mark, then in our response to an offence we must guard ourselves against the raw desire to make the offender suffer. The evolution of a public justice system as a replacement for personal responses to evil was intended to place an obstacle before the forward momentum of private revenge. Purging ourselves of hatred in responding to evil is not sentimentality or passivity The criminal justice system, the institution that responds on our behalf to those who have injured us, has to practise an emotionless objectivity. And it does this in the name of an ancient principle. Arendt was passionate about the importance of justice in responding to the chaotic forces that face the human community. In her account of Eichmann's trial she makes the point clear.

> I held and hold the opinion that this trial had to take place in the interests of justice and of nothing else . . . and in view of the current confusion in legal circles about the meaning and usefulness of punishment, I was glad that the judgment quoted Grotius, who, for his part, citing an older author, explained that punishment is necessary 'to defend the honour or the authority of him who was hurt by the offence so that failure to punish may not cause his degradation'.[26]

The nature of the punishment is not itself the issue here, and can be widely varied in concept and execution; it is the fact that the person who was hurt by the offence was, in the language of Grotius, degraded, that is important here. Degradation is another way of saying the injured party had been turned into a thing and therefore violated at the very core of her humanity. This is why there is a fundamental need in people who have been abused to have that fact acknowledged and proclaimed. Gobodo-Madikizela's experience in South Africa's Truth and Reconciliation Commission proved to her the importance of what we might call the performative rhetoric of justice. She says that a genuine apology is a 'speech act' designed to right the relationship damaged through the actions of the apologiser. The apology cannot, of course, erase what was done, but it has the potential to transform the situation created by the offence. In order to work, the apologiser has to name the deed, acknowledge the wrongdoing, recognise and in some sense feel the pain of the victim.[27]

Here Gobodo-Madikizela emphasises an aspect of justice that is insufficiently observed in the justice systems of Britain and the US: the needs of the victim. Western justice has been good at limiting the momentum of force by institutionalising its response to offenders who, in theory, are judged dispassionately in order to express humanity's disapproval of those who turn against it. What we have paid less attention to is the trauma caused to the victim who needs, for her own re-integration after degradation, to hear the offender 'perform' his acknowledgement of the wrong done. In some cultures this act *is* the punishment of the offender, who is brought back within the human community he turned against once he has sincerely owned the reality of what he did, has performed an adequate apology and made some form of restitution. There is growing evidence that the 'performance' of repentance has a greater chance of re-integrating offenders into the community than the imposition of other types of punishment. Unfortunately, the momentum of the justice systems in the US and Britain is running counter to this insight, with the paradoxical effect that it tends to increase rather than correct criminality. Its promiscuous use of prison as punishment is closer to the ugly desire to cause pain to the offender than to Arendt's claim that the purpose of justice is the recognition that the person offended must have her humanity restored by an act that recognises her degradation. That is the first and fundamental element in a wise justice system. The second must be to try to find ways to restore the offenders to the human community they have turned against. Unfortunately, most of the punishment regimes in Britain and the US, especially the increasingly automatic use of imprisonment, only fortifies the evil and alienation of the prisoner. Of course, there will always be people who have turned so utterly against their own kind that they must be permanently separated from their fellows. Hannah Arendt, who supported the execution of Eichmann, expressed this necessity in words she wishes his judges had addressed to him:

> Just as you supported and carried out a policy of not wanting to share the earth with the Jewish people and the people of a number of other nations – as though you and your superiors had any right to determine who should and who should not inhabit the world – we find that no one, that is, no member of the human race, can be expected to want to share the earth with you.[28]

The mystery of evil will probably always require us to make judgements like that, but we must never delude

ourselves about how, in the right circumstances, we ourselves might have found ourselves on the wrong road.
Just as importantly, in our struggle against evil we must
be careful not to let our own hearts be turned to stone
by the pain we have suffered. That is why Simone Weil
wants us to be aware of force's indifference to the human
cost of its momentum, from the siege of Troy to the
destruction of Fallujah; just as it is indifferent to the fate
of the disordered children with whom we presently fill
our gaols. It is using us all, presiding at the feast of
hatred, turning us all to stone. Artists see this with greater
clarity than the politicians who fancy themselves as men
of destiny propelling history forward, whereas they
themselves are being driven like leaves before a gale in
autumn.

If we can derive anything from these explorations
it is that being human is not easy. Consciousness and
the apparent possession of free will incline us to believe
that we have control over our lives, but the facts would
suggest something rather different. It is as though we
had been given the keys to a powerful automobile
and set off along the motorway only to discover that,
while we have some control of the vehicle, it also
seems to be subject to other forces. It makes sudden
and unforeseen manoeuvres, takes dangerous swerves into
oncoming traffic, and sometimes stops for no obvious
reason, engine still running, and refuses to move another
inch. We do have some control over our lives, but there
are other influences at work in us, not of our choosing,
hardly even of our knowing, that exercise considerable
power over us. Obviously, there is the great flow of the

life force itself and its determination to keep going, regardless of the consequences to those it has elected as its vehicles. We are certainly more than gene-replicating devices, but that is also what we are. And while we are theoretically in charge of our own character and its development, much of it is programmed by forces over which we never could have had any control. Apart from the unsearchable memory of the human species that lies deep within us, each of us was thrown into a unique and specific life-context, the earliest stages of which had profound effects, for good or ill, on our subsequent history. We are also strangely subject to the gravitational pull of the human herd. Sometimes the consequences of this magnetic force are endearingly pathetic, such as the need to have the latest fashion accessory or the most versatile mobile phone; but sometimes the consequences are truly terrifying. The human herd, when collectively aroused, is the most ferocious beast on the planet. It is responsible for every lynching, every gang-bang, every act of genocide, every heresy hunt, every ugly bout of group thinking that has ever afflicted the human community. Sadly, there always seem to be charismatic monsters around who are brilliant at rousing the herd and hypnotising it into obedient servitude to their terrifying visions. Fortunately, there also seem to be a few rare individuals who are impervious to all the pressures I have described. As I shall attempt to show, these alone are capable of consistently speaking the truth and naming the lie. The rest of us crowd ourselves uncertainly between the monsters and the martyrs: strangely attracted to the magnetism of the villain, yet made wistful by the courage of the saint. History would suggest that we are more susceptible to the seductive power of the monster than the fierce challenge of the saint. But I shall argue that history also teaches that we can come to an understanding of the tragic complexity of the human condition and work to mitigate the damage we do to one another. The way to begin the turnaround is by telling the truth about ourselves to ourselves. Radical honesty about ourselves is the ground in which pity can flower.

2

PITY

Yonder he is through the stream, a man without a coat, a man without a belt, a man of hard slender legs, it is my woe that I cannot run.

IRISH RIDDLE

From 1970 to the summer of 1980 when we left Scotland for North America, we owned a cottage at Muckhart Mill, a couple of miles outside Dollar in Clackmannanshire. For those ten years we spent a month there every summer, with visits for a few days at other times, and the odd snatched weekend. It was only an hour's drive from Edinburgh, so we often went up for the day in the good weather, if only to cut the grass and pick some roses. It became a valuable retreat from a busy city rectory. The cottage was called 'Pathend', and my father-in-law, who loved to stay there when he visited us from the USA, wrote a poem about it.

> After the city streets, a country lane,
> After the noisy world, the quiet hills.
> Instead of tramping feet, a running stream:
> Instead of troubled hearts, the gift of peace.
> Beyond the paths that wander without end,
> I turn to you – my hearth, my home, my friend.

The beauty of spending long summer weeks at 'Pathend' was that we got into a rhythm that had the feel of living, rather than holidaying. We swam in the River Devon; we walked in the Ochil Hills; and the children and I cycled all over to find wild raspberries that my wife Jeannie made into the best jam in the world. And on the finest day of the summer we took a special picnic up Dollar Glen. We chose the best day deliberately, because the glen, as its name suggests, can be a dolorous place. On a grey day it was sorrowful, and subdued us with its ancient memories; but on the fine sunny days we chose it was mysterious rather than sad, contemplative rather than forbidding. We would come out at Castle Campbell for our picnic, before following the path beside Burn of Care up onto Whitewisp Hill, where we would turn round and look with full hearts at all of broad Scotland. I can see it now, as I write, and my children beside me.

There was a particular poignancy about planning the 1980 hike, because it would be our last. At the end of August we were moving to Boston, Massachusetts, where I was to take up a new post. 'Pathend' had been sold, and the new owners were to move in on the morning of our departure. The saddest memory I have of that pensive summer is of the terrible fight our border terrier Kip had with the dog at the mill down the lane. We hadn't realised it was going on till it was almost over, when she was so exhausted with the struggle she could hardly move. I found her in the middle of the path that ran down to the farm, lying on her side bleeding, panting uncontrollably, and I carried her back to the house. I still wonder if that was when the cancer started working in her. She was twelve, getting on for a dog, but that summer she was still as determined an accomplice as ever on our hikes in the hills and swims in the river. She and Tigger the cat were tranquillised for the flight across the Atlantic and emerged groggy but inquisitive into the Boston sunshine, where they quickly adapted themselves to the new scene.

We were surprised by the severity of our first winter in New England. On Christmas Day we were able to walk over the thick ice on the pond in Boston's Public Garden, and Kip picked up her paws and shook them after each step, unable to believe how cold it was. Early in the New Year we discovered that she was riddled with cancer. She was operated on at the local veterinary hospital, but it was obvious that she could not long survive. As tolerant and sweet-natured as ever, she tried to take part in our lives with her accustomed enthusiasm, though every move was clearly agony. I can remember the puzzled look she gave me when her body refused any longer to respond to her will, and I realised it was all over for her. The hospital advised us to bring her in the following after-noon, when they would mercifully end her life. What neither of us can forgive ourselves for is that we did not accompany her into the room where they killed her. We took her to Reception and handed her over. Grief-stricken, we watched them take her through to the back, then we walked to the parking lot, got into our car and drove home without her. We owed her a gentle and painless death, but we also owed her our presence beside her at the end, and we failed her. It is the absoluteness of such failure that is devouring: absolute, because death rules out any possibility of retrieving or redeeming the failure.

We returned to Britain four years after Kip's death and acquired Sam, another border terrier. He was a tougher customer than Kip, and outlived her by a couple of years. Inevitably, time caught up with him as well. He became blind, deaf and incontinent. Almost till the end he was game for a walk round the familiar streets of Edinburgh, but it was heartbreaking to see him bump against kerbstones and stumble into lampposts. The day came when the kindly neighbourhood vet suggested that his time was over and I should bring him in whenever I felt up to it. On the morning of the decision I tried to give him a bit of a last walk, but he was so weak and bewildered that I had to carry him. I cradled in my arms the small, muscular body that had finally betrayed him, and took him to his final appointment at Mr Hunter's. This time I was determined to stay. I placed him on his side on the table in the clinic, and continued to stroke him as the vet, with enormous gentleness, tranquillised him. Then he gave him the lethal injection; and with a small forgiving sigh Sam was gone. I stumbled home, blinded by tears, and Jeannie and I fell into each other's arms and wept. Kip and Sam were part of the history of our family, their short lives wound round our own; now they exist only in our memories and in some old photographs. Animal lovers soon become acquainted with grief, which is the amazed protest of life at the fact of death. Leonard Woolf remembered being told, when he was a boy, to drown five new-born puppies.

When he plunged the first tiny blind creature into the bucket of water, it began 'to fight desperately for its life, struggling, beating the water with its paws'. He suddenly realised that it was an individual, an 'I', and that it was fighting for its life just as he would, were he drowning. 'It was,' he wrote at the very end of his long life, 'a horrible, an uncivilized thing to drown that "I" in a bucket of water.'[29]

The Book of Common Prayer says that 'in the midst of life we are in death.'[30] This may be less obvious to those of us who live in highly urbanised communities, where our alienation from nature is almost complete, and where the medicalisation of our lives has distanced us even from our own dying. How animals understand dying may be impossible for us to figure, but they certainly grieve. Elephants grieve a long time, and so do whales. Many birds that lose a mate will never take another one. A friend of mine had a cat who, on losing her companion, sat on the stairs and cried without ceasing. Dogs, being pack animals, are more robust about the coming and going of other pack members. But when they lose their pack leader they mourn deeply. Because the human is the pack leader where dogs are kept as pets, the death of their master can devastate them. There are many stories of the Greyfriars Bobby kind, about broken-hearted dogs who remained faithful till death to a lost master. Animals are not oblivious to death, and have their own way of protesting against the last enemy, the runner who is always just behind us.[31] Loren Eiseley captured one moment of protest perfectly:

When I awoke, dimly aware of some commotion and outcry in the clearing, the light was slanting down through the pines in such a way that the glade was lit like some vast cathedral. I could see the dust motes of wood pollen in the long shaft of light, and there on the extended branch sat an enormous raven with a red squirming nestling in its beak.

The sound that awoke me was the outraged cries of the nestling's parents, who flew helplessly in circles about the clearing. The sleek black monster was indifferent to them. He gulped, whetted his beak on the dead branch a moment and sat still. Up to that point the little tragedy had followed the usual pattern. But suddenly, out of all that area of woodland, a soft sound of complaint began to rise. Into the glade fluttered small birds of half a dozen varieties drawn by the anguished cries of the tiny parents.

No one dared to attack the raven. But they cried there in some instinctive common misery, the bereaved and the unbereaved. The glade filled with their soft rustling and their cries. They fluttered as though to point their wings at the murderer. There was a dim intangible ethic he had violated, that they knew. He was a bird of death. And he, the murderer, the black bird at the heart of life, sat on there, glistening in the common light, formidable, unperturbed, untouchable.[32]

Nature is ruthless, and Eiseley's picture of that enormous raven, with a red squirming nestling in its beak, captures the grimness of it. It may be splendid in its implacable ferocity, but it is also stunning in its indifference. Half of all polar bear cubs die in their first year. The Kalahari kills the young elephants that try to cross it in search of water. And throughout the animal kingdom predators stalk their victims before launching

themselves for the paralysing kill. In the midst of life
we *are* in death. It is the pitilessness of the natural order
that fortifies the atheist against any idea of the existence of a benevolent creator. This was something that
Darwin observed, though he was himself too benevolent to assume the role he described: 'What a book a
devil's chaplain might write on the clumsy, wasteful,
blundering, low, and horribly cruel works of nature.'[33]
The fact is that nature is a vast food-chain and killing
is as intrinsic to its purpose as sex. The fight is as fundamental as the fuck. The life that stuttered into being
billions of years ago in that sea of chemicals battles not
only to replicate itself, but to maintain itself, mainly
by preying on other creatures. The explorer Benedict
Allen gives a vivid snapshot of the way one species
lives off another, including the human. He came across
a German hermit living in the rainforest who struggled to eke out an existence from that formidable
habitat. Asked what would happen if he got ill, he
replied:

'In this *unlikely* case, there is, of course, my larder . . .'
He pointed to the brook that flowed through the
camp. Beyond the mud bank I saw a piece of string,
and at the end of it were his emergency rations: a
quietly grazing tortoise.
'Surely you'd eat him only for a feast?' I said.
'On the contrary: only when I might die. It is my
agreement with him.'
'Agreement?'
'Or should I say it is the tortoise's agreement with
nature. He is granted life, but on condition that one

day his life may be taken by something higher in the food chain. And I,' he added with what seemed to me was triumph, 'am higher in the food chain.'[34]

The hermit's lack of sentimentality about his tortoise exactly captures the tragic reality of life. The tiny birds that protested against the murderous activity of the giant raven were themselves killers of forms of life that make less appeal to our emotions: insects, worms, grubs, snails. Anyone who has watched a blackbird bash the shell of a snail on a rock to uncover and consume the living creature hiding within it will be cured of any sentimentality towards nature, even in its more winsome forms. Nevertheless, there is a kind of rough justice in nature. While it may be disputable whether an intentional regulatory intelligence lies behind it, nature operates in a way that maintains the multiplicity of species in some kind of balance. The raven devours the nestlings, but some survive to live out their natural span. If this were not so, the dominant species, the violent raptors and hunters, would destroy their own means of survival. Nature red in tooth and claw may not be a pretty sight, but there is a balance to it, even what we might describe as a kind of ecological justice.

Or there was, till we humans destroyed the balance. Eiseley describes the raven as the murderer, the black bird at the heart of life, but the description ought more justly to be attached to the human, the promiscuous destroyer, the true murderer in the forest. As our propensity for dreaming up imaginative systems of torture reminds us, we have been highly inventive in our cruelty towards members of our species. Of course, we have never been reluctant to torture the other animals with whom we share the planet either – as the history of our cruelty to them clearly shows – but until fairly recently we were limited in our ability to interfere in their lives by the means at our disposal. Though we started damaging the atmosphere of the earth and meddling with its systems centuries ago, we maintained some elements of justice in the balance between ourselves and the other animals. A good example was the poise achieved between the Plains tribes of North America and the massive herds of bison or buffalo that roamed the Great Plains from Canada to Mexico. The nineteenth-century United States Government understood this symbiosis, and in order to further its expansion into the West, promoted organised bison-hunting to starve out the population of the Plains Indians. As a result, the bison was hunted almost to extinction. The irony is that as a result of wise conservation policies today, the American bison or buffalo has made an astonishing comeback, but it is far too late to revive the horse culture of the Plains Indians.

Hunting is the instinctive technique of the natural predator, but we, the most intelligent of them, discovered that our lives would be easier and less perilous if we farmed rather than hunted the animals we depended on for food. Like the German hermit in the rainforest, we decided to keep our larder close at hand. Even so, a raw justice was maintained. The animals we husbanded had their time on hill and field till the moment we slaughtered them. On the appointed day they would sense their impending death and protest against it, as life instinctively does; but their dying would be quickly accomplished by the hands that had husbanded them in the place in which they had lived their lives. In his meditation 'Why Look at Animals?' John Berger captures the complex nature of the affection between farmer and animal in traditional society.

> A peasant becomes fond of his pig and is glad to salt away its pork. What is significant, and is so difficult for the urban stranger to understand, is that the two statements in that sentence are connected by an *and*, not by a *but*.'[35]

Berger says that the nineteenth century in Western Europe and North America saw the beginning of a process that was completed in our day by twentieth-century corporate capitalism, ' by which every tradition which has previously mediated between man and nature was broken. Before this rupture, animals constituted the first circle of what surrounded man.'[36] Modern industrial farming has changed that relationship. The animals who are the objects of our greedy domination experience a double-dying now, their life being itself a kind of death. The existence we grudgingly allow them is a crowded disease-prone torture, before we pack them onto death trucks and transport them hundreds of miles to licensed slaughterhouses. The sense of the tragic interconnectedness of our relationship to animals, characterised by Berger's peasant and his pig, has been destroyed by the factory farming methods our greed has evolved.

I know a doctor who keeps a special breed of sheep as a hobby. He knows all thirty of them individually, just as they, he claims, know each other, sheep being by no means the silly creatures we imagine them to be. In a decent society he would slaughter his sheep at home, when the time came, the way Berger's peasant killed his pig, the way farmers have done for centuries. It distresses the sheep-loving doctor to have to load his beloved flock onto transporters that truck them to a state-licensed abattoir, heavy with the smell of death and noisy with the protest of animals who know they are about to be fed into its killing machine. Our gluttony and contempt of the other animals with whom we share the earth has led us into monstrous behaviour. Since 1961, livestock has increased worldwide by 38%, to about 4.3 billion. The global population of birds has quadrupled in that time, to 17.8 billion, and the number of pigs has trebled to 2 billion. This enormous increase in such a short period has totally changed our relationship with the animals we rely on for food. Danielle Nierenberg, a researcher with the US Worldwatch Institute, has warned us that, 'Raising animals has morphed into an industrial endeavour that bears little relation to landscape or natural tendencies of the animals.' She points out that wherever industrial farming is introduced it creates ecological and public health disasters.[37] Animal overpopulation leads to disease. In their natural environment animals are rarely crowded together in an unsustainable way because of the balance the natural food-chain achieves, but in the hellish conditions of factory farms they spend their lives packed together like rush-hour commuters in underground trains.

Confining animals like this leads to physical problems, such as osteoporosis and joint pain, as well as boredom and frustration, shown by repetitive and self-destructive behaviour. In short, before killing them we drive them mad. This is why hours after their birth in battery hen complexes, chickens have their beaks sliced off with a hot blade to prevent them pecking each other to death as they crowd against each other.

Apart from the horrors of the double-dying we now inflict on the animals we keep in our global larders, we are deservedly stoking up an eschatological night-mare for ourselves. Our addiction to intensive food production, and its attendant excesses, has generated an epidemic of obesity and other self-induced diseases. And nature itself has been corrupted and diseased by our greed and cruelty. In 1996 the link between the cattle disease bovine spongiform encephalopathy (BSE) and its human equivalent, Creutzfeldt-Jakob disease (CJD), was reported. Five years later, anyone travelling in the springtime through rural Britain saw hecatombs blazing on green hills, as the Government battled to stop the spread of foot-and-mouth disease. Seven million sheep and cattle were destroyed before the spread of the disease was halted.

At the time of the great slaughter, there were stories of farmers who by night deliberately drove healthy cattle into infected herds so that they could get Government compensation, which was more profitable for them than honest farming. One of the most harrowing images from those days was of sheep trying to escape from the flocks of death, being hunted down by farmers and

clumsily executed as they ran. Robert Crawford captured
this macabre reversal in a poem:

> I am the bad shepherd, torching my flocks in the
>   fields,
> Feeding them accelerant, hecatombs of wedders
>   and tups.
> In pits or pyres all are sheared and shamed by the
>   flames . . .
> I am the bad shepherd. Follow me.[38]

And as I write this hundreds of thousands of turkeys are
being slaughtered at the Bernard Matthews 'farm' in Suffolk
in an attempt to quell the spread of the virulent H5N1
or avian influenza among the enclosed flock. One of the
most poignant aspects of the latest scare is the occasional
glimpses television news cameras have given us into the
enormous windowless sheds, where we can see thousands
of turkeys crammed together, deprived of anything
remotely describable as a life, before they are sent off to
the execution chamber to satisfy our craving for cheap
food. Claudia Tarry, a campaigner against the turkey trade,
was able to get into a Bernard Matthews' barn one night,
and has provided us with a description of the horror she
found. When she slid open the door of the enormous
turkey barn she was hit by the stench of stale warm air,
excreta and ammonia. No daylight or fresh air. Everywhere
the hum of ventilators and the noise of 20,000 turkeys,
shuffling from foot to foot, pecking at dry pellets in the
automatic feeders, sipping water from the drinking bells,
each confined to an area the size of the roasting tin that
was to be their final destination. Built into the economics

of the system is the concept of the 'starve out', hundreds of thousands of birds who can't make it to the feeders or drinking bells and die of starvation or thirst. Dead or dying birds were lying around the barn she entered. The most surreal discovery was the masturbation shed, a small building divided into several pens, each enclosing eight male turkeys. The shed contained a single chair with an attached vice, and an arrangement of tubes, funnels, pumps and phials. In order to masturbate the stags every few days, they are held in the vice while having their sex glands stimulated. The semen is then milked into a tube and injected into the female. The stags were huge, unwieldy birds, with bald patches on wings and feathers from being repeatedly held in the masturbation vice. When they attempted to move they wobbled painfully and laboriously. In this single complex there were over fifty barns, each a nightmarish replica of the other.[39] Grim establishments like this are dotted all over the British countryside. I see one regularly from the window of the train that commutes between Edinburgh and Glasgow, and I wonder at the misery it represents, the thoughtless cruelty it proclaims. Long rows of wooden windowless sheds, with the look of a place that has something to hide. What is hidden is the industrialised torture of tens of thousands of birds, artificially created to live artificial lives before they are slaughtered for our consumption. No longer is there any sense that they belong to nature and deserve a life, however brutish or short it might be. Now, they are *product*, their status as living creatures an awkward but necessary interlude in their painful journey to our supermarket shelves and fast-food outlets.

As I have already suggested, the most disturbing things about the human species is our ability to accustom ourselves to monstrous behaviour. We have accommodated ourselves to death camps and industrialised genocide. Recently we re-accommodated ourselves to the practice of torture done in our name. Nevertheless, we debate these matters and sometimes even shame ourselves into repentance. But few of us appear to be perturbed by the torment we inflict on the creatures we depend on for our own survival. Nature is undoubtedly ruthless, but our genius as a species is to have refined cruelty with such scientific precision as to make nature seem benign in comparison. In its raw state nature gives all animals a fighting chance of surviving the struggle of life till death grabs them in its raven's beak. If death itself is the chief predator of the great killers, nature has endowed the others with a complex armoury of defensive capability: speed, disguise, odour, poison. We have disturbed the order of nature and assumed absolute power over it; and we have given ourselves divine warrant for doing so.

> And God said, Let us make man in our image, after our likeness: and let them have dominion over the fish of the sea, and over the fowl of the air, and over the cattle, and over all the earth, and over every creeping thing that creepeth upon the earth.[40]

The dominion we have assumed over the animal kingdom has been catastrophic for ourselves as well as for them. In his book *The Dominion of the Dead*, Robert

Pogue Harrison discusses Eleanor Wilner's poem 'Reading the Bible Backwards', in which she envisions the reversal or undoing of the Creation story from Genesis. 'What [the poem] describes is a redemption, not of history but of nature, a redemption that takes the form of a universal flood that would "reverse the spell" of human history's disasters and tragedies.' This is the conclusion of the poem:

Now nothing but the wind
moves in the rain-pocked face
of the swollen waters, though far below
where the giant squid lie hidden in shy tangles,
the whales, heavy-bodied as angels,
their fins like vestiges of wings,
sing some mighty epic of their own –

a great day when ships would all withdraw,
the harpoons fail of their aim, the land
dissolve into the waters, and they would swim
among the peaks of the mountains, like
eagles of the deep, while far below them, the old
nightmares of earth would settle
into silt among the broken cities, the empty
basket of the child would float
abandoned in the seaweed until the work of water
unravelled it in filaments of straw,
till even that straw rotted
in the planetary thaw the whales prayed for,
sending their jets of water skyward
in the clear conviction they'd spill back
to ocean with their will accomplished
in the miracle of the rain. *And the earth*
was without form and void, and darkness

was upon the face of the deep. And
the Spirit moved upon the face of the waters.

Harrison says:

> The form the earth takes under the dominion of humans
> brings only death and enslavement to its other crea-
> tures, and mostly misery to the offenders. For Wilner
> the sins of the seed of Adam are sins against nature,
> not God, hence the guilt of history is neither punish-
> able nor atonable. It is only oblivionable through the
> miracle of the rain.[41]

Who knows? Maybe nature is plotting its revenge against
us for bringing death and enslavement to its midst, and
one day our species will be swept to oblivion by the
miracle of the rain, letting evolution run itself again, this
time stopping before the emergence of our murderous
species. If the planet has achieved self-consciousness and
volition in us, its most profligate children, why is it
impossible to believe that it may possess a profound intelligence of its own, and may be in the process of shaking
us off the way a dog shakes water off its coat? One of
the dark myths from our own childhood anticipated this
idea of expulsion from a garden we had ruined by our
discontent. When our imagination was weaving the great
truth-bearing myths it was already mourning our addiction to death and anticipating our own tragic history.
'Now the serpent was more subtil than any beast of the
field which the Lord God had made. And he said unto
the woman, Yea, hath God said, Ye shall not eat of every
tree of the garden?'[42] According to the Genesis Creation

myth, from the beginning we resisted the balance and fairness of nature. Not content with our stewardship of the beasts and the liberality of the gift of 'every herb bearing seed, which is upon the face of all the earth, and every tree, in which is the fruit of a tree yielding seed',[43] we overreached and banished ourselves from the good life, the life according to the tragic mutuality of nature. 'And God saw that the wickedness of man was great in the earth, and that every imagination of the thoughts of his heart was only evil continually. And it repented the Lord that he had made man on the earth, and it grieved him at his heart.'[44]

To compound our folly, not only have we separated ourselves from nature, we have cut ourselves off from the power our myths possess to alert us to the danger of our own excesses. Nietzsche understood the profundity of this loss:

> For it is the lot of all myths to creep gradually into the confines of a supposedly historical reality, and to be treated by some later age as unique fact with claims to historical truth . . . this is how religions tend to die: the mythic premises of a religion are systematized, beneath the stern and intelligent eyes of an orthodox dogmatism, into a fixed sum of historical events; one begins nervously defending the veracity of myths, at the same time resisting their continuing life and growth. The feeling for myth dies and is replaced by religious claims to foundation in history.[45]

We have lost the feeling for myth, the dark poetry of our unremembered past, and replaced it with the fraudulent

veracity of religious claims 'to historical reality'. This
accounts for the peculiar ugliness of both religious and
anti-religious protagonists today, neither of whom has any
feel for the creative power of metaphor. By literalising it,
either in the name of the dogmatic orthodoxies of religion or the dismissive orthodoxies of science, we have
cut ourselves off from the ability of myth to hold a mirror
in front of ourselves. The old myths of our Creation and
Expulsion from Eden, woven when we hardly knew the
difference between ourselves and the rest of nature, can
still illuminate the tension in our own souls, pulled between
sympathy for other living creatures and cold indifference
to them.

Trying to imagine ourselves back into the consciousness from which the ancient myths emerged can be a
useful and revealing exercise. We discover fear of an
underlying chaos that lurks in the depths of the human
psyche, and from which we have sought to separate
and distance ourselves. In Genesis there is a Hebrew
verb that captures the essence of this anxiety: *hivdil*,
divide. 'And God said, Let there be light: and there was
light. And God saw the light, that it was good: and God
divided the light from darkness.'[46] According to the myth,
it is by division that creation is brought out of the
confusion of chaos: light from darkness, day from night,
dry land from the frightening deep. One of humanity's
fears is of a return to the undivided state, to chaos. In
traditional religion this anxiety has translated itself into
codes of division and separation covering every aspect
of life: foods that are forbidden, forms of sexual
encounter that are banned, and contagious engagement

with other peoples and tribes that is prohibited. Though the secular mind is baffled by these injunctions, they are an example of an ancient fear of things falling apart and returning us to chaos. This is obviously a powerful element in the resurgence of conservative religion in the world today. One of the main drivers of the secular ideal has been the overthrowing of what it considers to be unjust divisions between humans, but the consequences appal the religious mind, the mind that divides and separates because it is fearful of the turbulence of the human id.

It is not easy to figure out why, in these ancient myths, we cast God in the role of separator, the one who divided order from chaos. Whether it comes from the unconscious memory of the evolutionary struggle encoded in our genes or from some other primordial anxiety, we have felt impelled to erect barriers against the floodwaters of our own tendency to chaos. The Freudian myth of the tripartite self – id in the flooded basement, representing churning chaotic desire; superego in the upper floor, representing the repressive anxiety of controlling authority; and ego, the conscious self, the bit we are aware of, caught in the middle between forces we don't understand and whose very existence we are unsure of – is a suggestive attempt at expressing the experience of the self. This is certainly what life can feel like. Religious institutions evolved partly to control and partly to embody these cloudy anxieties. This is why conservative religions are outraged by what they perceive to be the chaos of secular societies. The controlling authority of the religious superego has been overthrown, and the old dividing walls have been washed away. Men and women meet on equal terms, with a consequent sexualisation of culture that is anathema to the pre-secular mind. It is in the area of sexuality that the most dramatic departure from the old culture of separation is seen. That is why those religious forms that have been most influenced and modified by secular thinking, such as liberal Protestantism, are in turmoil today as traditionalists fight to regain control of institutions they believe have been corrupted. And it is why conservative Muslims are seeking to re-establish the symbols of the old divisions, such as the *hijab*, within the open spaces of secular society.

It is not surprising that from a nature as complex as ours have come forth myths and archetypes that divide us not only from one another, but from the other animals with whom we share the earth. Is the human 'I' different in kind and destiny from the animal 'I', and is this why we have assumed absolute authority over it? Certainly, the Creation myth in Genesis asserted that there was a qualitative difference between us and the other creatures with whom we share the earth: 'And God said, Let us make man in our image, after our likeness . . . So God created man in his own image, in the image of God created he him; male and female created he them.'[47] Do we treat animals with cruelty because we believe that they are so qualitatively different from us as to be little more than animate machines? The ancient creation myths were all formed before we knew anything about our common origin, so it is inevitable that they emphasised the difference rather than the similarity between us and the other animals. It will probably remain impossible for us ever to know what the animal 'I' feels like. Though we know that many species, from ants to whales, have sophisticated communication systems, it is hard to know whether they experience anything like our self-consciousness. Nevertheless, as Leonard Woolf realised when he plunged a blind puppy in a bucket of water, it was an individual, an 'I', and it was fighting for its life just as he would, were he drowning. The sense we have of the importance of our own identity, our own 'I', should predispose us towards according the animal 'I' some sympathy and respect. After all, it is the 'I' within the human entity that gave us our first experience of transcendence and is the most likely origin of the religious sense: the possibility that there may be a superabundant, trans-human 'I' behind the mystery of things. Myth was our first attempt at grappling with these mysteries. Acknowledging that it comes from our infancy as a species is not to denigrate it, it is to offer it the tribute of a true understanding of its significance. Myth is art, not the fixed historical truth of dogmatic religion; it tells us about *ourselves*, not some trans-historical reality about which we can only guess. Robert Hughes, the art critic, meditating on human creativity, says: 'It has been said, often and truthfully, that genius is nothing other than the ability to recapture childhood at will – but this has to include the terrors and desires of childhood, not just its Arcadian innocence.'[48] We can see this if we closely observe young children playing on their own, conjuring up populations, mysteries, dangers, singing the world into meaning. While most of us clamp a heavy lid over the well of our imagination when we emerge from childhood, the artist goes on drawing from it at will. If we are to learn from myth, the art of our early imagination as a species, we must ask ourselves: if these are the stories we told ourselves, what were the pressures that prompted them? When we put the question that way, a number of puzzles confront us. One is the existential status of the other animals with whom we share the earth. The answer we gave to that question has had terrible consequences for these other creatures; but our problematic response may itself be a consequence of answers we have given to other questions, questions that address the conundrum of our own existence. When news of his daughter Aline's death of pneumonia finally reached Paul Gauguin in Tahiti in 1897 he produced a massive painting that was a cry of pain at the mystery of existence. He wrote three questions on a corner of the canvas: *D'Où Venons-Nous?* Where do we come from? *Que Sommes-Nous?* What are we? *Où Allons-Nous?* Where are we going? Though we have been largely incurious about the inner lives of the other animals and what sense, if any, they have of themselves, we have been massively curious about our own nature and destiny. Linking these opposing responses has been the conviction that the human 'I' differs fundamentally from the animal 'I'. It is Death, the prompter in the wings, that has parsed that distinction, by inciting us to speculate about the possibility that, unlike the other animals, we possess immortal souls.

II
MARKET PLACE

3
SOUL

Never again, no matter how long I look out of the window, will I see your tall thin figure walking across the park past the dwarf pine past the stumps, and then climb the ha-ha and come across the lawn. Our jokes have gone for ever.

CARRINGTON

One day, a few weeks after my mother died, I was so overwhelmed by grief as I passed a spiritualist church advertising a service that I went in. It was not my first encounter with spiritualism. One of the most vivid memories of my boyhood was watching my mother and three women friends, including my Aunt Cathy, use a homemade Ouija board. Sometimes called a spirit board, any flat surface inscribed with the letters of the alphabet and the ten digits can be used for the practice. The claim is that the moving planchette or indicator, over which the participants place their hands, is prompted by spirits of the dead to provide answers to questions asked by the group. On this occasion the improvised indicator was a small whisky glass. I can't remember the question that was put, but I remember being electrified by the answer, which suggested that someone who lived across the street would soon meet with a terrible accident. When the session was over I wanted to know why they didn't immediately warn the neighbour of her impending fate. Cathy laughed: 'Nuthin's gonie happen. It's only a game, a joke,' she said.

Nevertheless, I kept a watchful eye on the neighbour for a few days after the episode, but my interest waned as the weeks passed and nothing unusual happened.

One Sunday night years later, when I was a parish priest on the Royal Mile in Edinburgh, the warden of a university hall of residence up near the castle asked if I would drop what I was doing and come to see them. It was one of those high old tenements at the top of the Mile, recently converted to student accommodation. I was told that a group of students had been having a jokey session with a Ouija board when the room suddenly became deadly cold and they were frightened out of their wits. By this time I knew the stories about how Ouija sessions could expose players to uninvited spiritual forces. I had no particular view on what had or had not happened, but I was enough of a pastoral pragmatist to know that I had to respond to the situation. We stood in that icy room and I prayed that whatever had entered should leave and peace should return. Normality was restored, the students were calmed, and I went home for my tea.

My default position on puzzles like the Ouija board is Occam's razor: all things being equal, the simplest explanation is usually the best. Psychologists explain the movement of the planchette by the ideomotor effect: usually two or three people have one hand on the device, so no single person needs to apply much force for the group as a whole to make it move and for each individual to imagine it is moving on its own. But what happened to that *room* at the top of the Royal Mile? I have no idea, but I daresay there is a natural explanation for that too. And if there is not, I can live with the uncertainty without buying the claim that spirit-boarding pierces the membrane between this world and the next and exposes participants to attack by demons who manage to slip through the crack.

All this reminds us that fascination over the fate of the dead is an ancient and abiding human preoccupation. Carrington was unable to accept the fact that every day for the rest of her life Lytton Strachey would be away. Her response was not to chase after the consoling fantasy of contact with him through spiritualism, but calmly and methodically to kill herself. To this day, history is full of stories of humans trying to reach beyond the grave to their beloved dead, doing what I did that day as I entered the spiritualist church. I walked out immediately after I walked in, because I did not believe in the possibility of communicating with my dead mother; but the strength of the impulse staggered me and provided me with an insight into the grief and longing that give séances their enduring appeal. Caring for our beloved dead is a deeply ingrained impulse, but more than grief is going on. If it is hard enough to accept that their *jokes* have gone for ever, it is almost impossible to believe that the person who told them has gone, never to return.

> Thou'lt come no more,
> Never, never, never, never, never![49]

Lear's fivefold 'never' is one of the most affecting lines in literature, as losing a child is the most wrenching experience life can throw at us. But other losses stun us as well, even the death of a beloved old dog. Our incredulity in the face of death has prompted many answers to Gauguin's questions, not only about where we are going, but about the nature of ultimate reality. Indeed, it could be argued that it was death that first whispered the idea of God and the soul into our heads. Devastating though it is, grief has been one of the great engines of human creativity and genius. To wander the cities of the dead, with their sometimes confident, some-times wistful memorials, is to touch worlds of grief. The necropolis in Glasgow stands on a hill above the medieval cathedral. Built to memorialise the dead, it also serves as a reminder to the living that the man with the hard slender legs of the Irish riddle is never far away and could catch up with us at any moment. To me, even more moving are the war memorials, none more powerful than the Vietnam Veterans Memorial in Washington, DC. It was opened on 13th November, 1982 in the presence of more than 150,000 people.

> Wheelchairs, fatigues, old Army jackets and a sea of decor-ations followed the brass parade toward the park between the Lincoln Memorial and the Washington Monument. After the sundry speeches, when the fences guarding the memorial finally came down, there was a prolonged, uneasy silence as people surveyed the wall, approached it, touched it, walked along it, searched it for the names of fallen kin or comrades. One by one veterans began to break down. Strangers embraced, weeping in each other's arms. Mothers, fathers, wives, daughters, sons, rela-tives, and friends of the dead also broke down, and before

long the scene of spontaneous grief moved reporters and broadcasters to tears as well. [50]

Since that day the Vietnam Veterans Memorial has become the most visited monument in the United States. Part of its power has undoubtedly to do with the unresolved tensions associated with the Vietnam War, but Robert Pogue Harrison believes there is also something symbolic about

> . . . the solemn gravity of the wall – the encrypted presence of the dead – which seems to turn the deaths of those memorialised into a stubborn question. The silence with which it responds to this question gives the wall's inscribed black granite panels an almost overwhelming power of withholding. The irresistible need many visitors feel to touch a chiselled name, kiss it, talk to it, offer it flowers or gifts, leave it notes or letters, is evidence enough of the dead's private presence in the stone – a presence at once given and denied.[51]

More than any other memorial to the dead I have visited, it conjures up Dante's famous line: 'I wondered how death could have undone so many.'[52]

Harrison says that preoccupation with our dead so defines us as a species that it could be said that to be human is to bury. 'I would say that humans bury not simply to achieve closure and effect a separation from the dead but also and above all to humanize the ground on which they build their worlds and found their histories.' He quotes Vico as saying that burial of the dead was one of three 'universal institutions' of humanity – along with religion and matrimony – and that *humanitas* in Latin comes first and properly from *humando*, burying.[53] It is worth noting here that the word translated as 'man' in the King James Bible's version of the Creation myth is *adam*, a Hebrew pun on *adamah*, 'the soil'.[54] Whatever subsequent developments there were in thinking about the nature and origin of humanity, for the Bible we are first and foremost part of nature, from the soil and destined to return to it. This is why, when the coffin is lowered into the grave during the Christian burial service, the officiant pronounces the words, 'earth to earth, ashes to ashes, dust to dust'. Part of the impulse to bury our dead is rooted in our tenderness towards the bodies of those we have loved and lost, along with our need to perform an act of acknowledgement and separation. But there is also a pronounced need in us to return our dead to the elements from which they came, whether we bury them in the earth, burn them in the fire or send them into the depths of the sea. This is why the grief of those who have no corpse to dispose of is agonising. They have opportunity neither to confirm the deadness of their dead nor to express their shock at the absoluteness of what has happened. Death, the one incontrovertible absolute we encounter in life, is an utter loss, beyond any hope of recovery or return, and we need to express our amazement at what it has stolen from us.

Virginia Woolf called death 'the immitigable tree', the harsh reality that is beyond any softening: there was an 'I', whose life was woven into the fabric of my own being; now she is gone, cancelled, erased. And the questions fill the throat: how can she just vanish? Has she gone somewhere else? And is she now utterly and for ever beyond my reach? Humans are not the only animals on the planet who are devastated by the deaths of those near to them, but we are the only ones who solemnly enact rituals of departure and farewell; and we are the only ones who express their anguish in words, such as Neville's meditation on the death of Percival in Virginia Woolf's *The Waves*.

'He is dead,' said Neville. 'He fell. His horse tripped. He was thrown. The sails of the world have swung round and caught me on the head. All is over. The lights of the world have gone out. There stands the tree which I cannot pass.

'Oh, to crumple this telegram in my fingers – to let the light of the world flood back – to say this has not happened! But why turn one's head hither and thither? This is the truth. This is the fact. His horse stumbled; he was thrown. The flashing trees and white rails went up in a shower. There was a surge; a drumming in his ears. Then the blow; the world crashed; he breathed heavily. He died where he fell.

'Barns and summer days in the country, rooms where we sat – all now lie in the unreal world which is gone. My past is cut from me . . . Why try to lift my foot and mount the stair? This is where I stand; here, holding the telegram. The past, summer days and rooms where we sat, stream away like burnt paper with red eyes in it. Why meet and resume? Why talk and eat and make up other combinations with other people? From this moment I am solitary. No one will know me now . . . I will not lift my foot to climb the stair. I will stand for one moment beneath the immitigable tree . . . '[55]

Given our disbelief at the way death steals our loves from us, it is no surprise that we have developed rites and ceremonies to help us express our grief and internalise the reality of our loss. But traditional burial customs carry profounder implications than the need to say goodbye and pass under the tree into the solitary life beyond the immitigable loss. Something else of immense significance is being said. The Book of Common Prayer expresses it dramatically:

> O Almighty God, with whom do live the spirits of just men made perfect, after they are delivered from their earthly prisons: We humbly commend the soul of this thy servant into thy hands, as into the hands of a faithful Creator and most merciful Saviour; most humbly beseeching thee, that it may be precious in thy sight. Wash it, we pray thee . . . that whatsoever defilements it may have contracted in the midst of this earthly life through the lusts of the flesh, or the wiles of Satan, being purged and done away, it may be presented pure and without spot before thee.[56]

That prayer, though specific to the Christian theological tradition, contains an idea that grew out of the human refusal to accept the finality of death – the concept of the soul, which carries the conviction that, though our bodies may die, the essential essence of the person survives death and moves into another state of being. Whether or not we believe it ourselves, we tend to take the existence of the idea for granted (it has been around for so long), but how did it arise?

The most obvious thing we notice about the dead is that something that used to happen has stopped happening: they no longer breathe. That is probably

why, from the beginning of thinking about the mystery
of existence, the idea of the soul or inner essence of a
person, what makes them alive not dead, was related to
the ability to breathe. It is a tiny leap, therefore, to asso-
ciate the distinctive essence of a person with breath.
The Greek word is *psyche*, which derives from the verb
to cool or blow – the way one blows on a spoonful
of hot soup to cool it. *Psyche* is what makes us live,
gives us spirit, consciousness, vitality. This is the word
that is used to translate the Hebrew word *nephesh* from
the Creation story in Genesis 2.7: 'And the Lord God
formed man of the dust of the ground, and breathed
into his nostrils the breath of life; and man became a
living *soul*.' In the Latin Bible the word is translated as
anima. It is obvious that it is the presence of this mysterious force that makes us alive and its absence that makes
us dead; but we are no further forward in understanding
what, if anything, it is in itself or where it came from.
All we have done so far is give it a name: *nephesh*, *psyche*,
anima, *soul*. The verb bit is obvious: we do breathe, and
we know that when we stop breathing we stop being:
but is it legitimate to turn the verb into a noun, to
move from a function, something we do breathing,
being alive – to something we have or something we
are? Do we actually possess a *psyche* or *soul* that can be
thought of as in some sense separate from our living,
breathing body, and is a thing in itself? The next step
in the development of the idea may lie in the human
experience of self-consciousness, the sense we have that
we somehow transcend our bodies: surely there has to
be more to us than this corpse-in-the-making that is

our flesh. Sigmund Freud wondered if nature was not always trying to reach back through death to the pre-animate state from which it once departed.

> If we may reasonably suppose that every living thing dies – reverts to the inorganic – then we can only say that *the goal of all life is death*, or to express it retro-spectively: *the inanimate existed before the animate*. At some point or other, the attributes of life were aroused in non-living matter by the operation upon it of a force that we are still quite incapable of imagining. Perhaps it was a process similar in essence to the one that later, at a certain level of living matter, gave rise to consciousness.[57]

And just as consciousness gave rise to the experience of the transcendent self – and may in turn have prompted the idea of the existence of a transcendent super-self or God, who is both immanent in, yet transcendent beyond nature – so religious anthropology developed a picture of the human 'I' as immanent in the body yet essentially transcending it and enduring beyond its dissolution.

That is certainly how we started thinking about ourselves. We established a fundamental differentiation between body and soul. Sometimes this is just a way of talking about what matters most to us: character, personality, 'soul', the inner me, as distinct from and maybe even opposed to the physical, external aspect of myself. This important distinction reminds us again of the demeaning experience of being objectified, either by sex or violence. In these circumstances, when force of some sort is turning us into a thing, it is important to keep hold of this sense of self, an 'I–dentity' that is distinct from the body which is being abused. It only takes another tiny step for this distinction to become substantive. No longer just a way of *talking* about ourselves, we now *think* of ourselves as bifurcated, as dual: something that lasts inhabiting for a time something that dies. And it is religion that begins to express this duality most dramatically. We may *have* a body, but we *are* something more, something over–and–above the physical: 'Fear not them which kill the body, but are not able to kill the soul: but rather fear him which is able to destroy both soul and body in hell.'[58] How did we get from observing the obvious fact of a body that breathes and thinks to the claim that the breather and thinker is an entirely separate entity: one that never dies; and which, if not properly managed, can land us in hell?

Tracing this progression is far from being an exact science, but we can detect a number of milestones along the way. Dreaming is a good place to start. Dreams have puzzled us for centuries. There we are asleep, unconscious, dead to the world, yet wildly alive in our dreams. No wonder the Greek poet Pindar claimed that when the body was asleep the soul was awake. Nietzsche was in no doubt that the dream was the origin of the idea of the double self.

> The separation of body and soul . . . is related to the most ancient conception of the dream; also the assumption of a quasi-body of the soul, which is the origin of all belief in spirits and probably also of belief in

gods. 'The dead live on; for they appear to the living
in dreams;' this inference went unchallenged for many
thousands of years.[59]

Since there is little real data to go on, most of our
thinking about this matter has to be conjectural, and
what Nietzsche says sounds like a good guess to me.
Before the soul really took off in religious and philosophical thinking, it was thought of as a kind of ghost
in the human machine, here for a season, then – well,
where exactly? The earliest idea seemed to be that when
it left the body at death it went off to the abode of
departed spirits, called *Hades* in Greek, *Sheol* in Hebrew,
translated in the King James Bible as 'the grave' or 'the
pit': 'For the grave cannot praise thee, death cannot cele-
brate thee: they that go down into the pit cannot hope
for thy truth.'[60] At this early stage in thinking about it,
the afterlife was not a place of punishment; it was a
dreary retirement home whose electricity had been cut
off, a dismal waiting room in which nothing ever
happened. But it was from this bleak concept that the
full floridity of hell would evolve in the religious mind.

While hell was being built – but before it was up
and running and packing them in – another development, on the face of it a more humane one, took place.
This was the idea, most prominently associated with
Plato, that the soul pre-existed the human habitation in
which it was sentenced to spend time. It was the eternal,
incorporeal occupant of a human body, whose fate was
to be reborn constantly into humans. Transmigration of
souls, or metempsychosis, is a prominent feature of

Eastern thinking about the soul, and is the dominant view in Hindu religion, with variants in other religions, including versions of Buddhism. Like everything else in this area, it is an entirely speculative concept, but it is not without its moral attractions. For the kind of mind that finds the gross inequity of human affairs intolerable it offers ultimate justice. What the soul makes of itself in its current life determines the kind of habitation it will achieve in future lives. The better you live now, the further up the ladder you will get next time round, till you are finally released from the endless round of rebirths and are absorbed into the ultimate state. There is something attractively calibrated about this approach that compares favourably with the cut-and-dried finality of the idea of the Last Judgement that is such a pronounced feature in Christianity and Islam.

But not even Christianity has a single, coherent view of the soul and its ultimate destination. Unsurprisingly, the Roman Catholic Church has the clearest and most systematic approach: it is essentially a synthesis of Platonist and Hebrew ideas. In common with most Christians, Catholicism believes that a soul gets one life and faces a final judgement after death on how it was used. Depending on how it performed in this life, it faces an eternity in heaven or hell; though there is a half-way house in purgatory for those deemed to be reclaimable after further training, rather the way earthly courts sometimes spare drug addicts gaol if they will submit to a spell in a rehabilitation unit. Catholics are at their most Platonic in their understanding of the soul's transition to eternal life at death. Those Christians who are closer to the Hebrew idea of the human being as animated dust, rather than as an embodied soul, believe that at death the human is totally destroyed, body *and* soul, and returns to the inorganic state from which it was derived. But just as God had animated the dust in the first place by breathing life into lifeless matter, so from the lifeless dust of death will God raise the person to a new life. However, this new life will not be passed in the material but in the spiritual realm, necessitating a different kind of body or identity. Saint Paul put it like this:

> But some will say, How are the dead raised up? and with what body do they come? Thou fool, that which thou sowest is not quickened, except it die: And that which thou sowest, thou sowest not that body that shall be, but bare grain, it may chance of wheat, or of some other grain: But God giveth it a body as it hath pleased him, and to every seed his own body . . . So also is the resurrection of the dead . . . It is sown a natural body; it is raised a spiritual body.[61]

Though it is never easy to figure out what exactly Paul is getting at, this passage does not sound like official Catholic theology. Catholics, like Plato, believe in the undying autonomy of the soul and are quite specific about the moment of its creation. They hold that each soul comes into existence precisely at the moment of conception, at the fusing of the egg and sperm. It is not that God takes a pre-existent soul and plants it in the new human – pure Platonism – but that God manufactures a new soul for each human and plants it at the

exact moment of conception. This is the root of the
Catholic Church's implacable opposition to any form
of abortion. The naked eye may only be able to see a
microscopic cluster of cells at the moment of fusion,
smaller than the head of a pin, but for Catholic theology
that tiny speck already has an eternal soul. However,
the Catholic Church is on its own here, because other
religions that believe in the soul, including other versions
of Christianity, take a more gradualist approach to
ensoulment. In Greek Orthodoxy ensoulment happens
at twenty-one days, in Islam at forty, while in Judaism
it takes eighty days. All of this may seem to the secular
mind to be totally unverifiable, but beliefs about the
timing of ensoulment have a profound effect on attitudes not only to abortion, but to the morning-after
pill. If you believe that the fusion of sperm and egg
instantly creates an immortal soul, then taking the
morning-after pill is as tantamount to murder as abortion; whereas, for other religious traditions, since they
believe the soul does not appear till further into the
pregnancy, then early interventions, including early abor-
tions, are morally less problematic.

If we go immediately to the other end of the life-
cycle, Christianity is as inconsistent on the precise
moment of resurrection as it is on the timing of ensoulment. Some Christians believe that the soul goes to
sleep at death and stays in unconscious hibernation till
the last trump wakes it for the final judgement. The
belief that the bodies of the dead rise from their graves
to be judged on the last day had a powerful effect on
the burial customs of Christians. If you took the belief

literally it made cremation unthinkable, because it left
no body to be re-assembled at the moment of the last
trump. This was why in the Roman Empire, under the
influence of Christianity, cremation had been abandoned
by the fifth century CE. Cremation was not revived in
the West till the nineteenth century, but even then it
took Christian churches a long time to accept it. In
Roman Catholicism it was finally permitted by an
instruction from the Holy Office in 1963, but uneasiness
about it still prevails.

A variant on the view that the soul sleeps till the
grand awakening holds that the soul at the point of
death immediately becomes present at the end of time,
having rocketed through temporality without noticing.
The Catholic Church certainly brooks no eschatological delay. In perfect symmetry, it teaches that, just
as at the moment of conception the soul was created,
so at the moment of death it goes immediately to judgement; hence the ancient fear of dying suddenly and
unprepared. This means that at every moment we are
standing potentially on the brink of the final Assize.
Shakespeare got the general theology right in Hamlet's
soliloquy when he decides to kill his hated stepfather,
whom he has discovered at prayer:

> Now might I do it pat, now he is praying;
> And now I'll do't: − and so he goes to heaven;
> And so am I reveng'd: − that would be scanned:
> A villain kills my father; and, for that,
> I his sole son, do this same villain send
> To heaven.
> O, this is hire and salary, not revenge.

He took my father grossly, full of bread;
With all his crimes broad blown, as flush as May;
And how his audit stands who knows save heaven?
But, in our circumstance and course of thought,
'Tis heavy with him: and am I, then, revenged,
To take him in the purging of his soul,
When he is fit and seasoned for his passage?
No.
Up, sword; and know thou a more horrid hent:
When he is drunk asleep, or in his rage;
Or in th' incestuous pleasure of his bed;
At gaming, swearing; or about some act
That has no relish of salvation in't; –
Then trip him, that his heels may kick at heaven;
And that his soul may be as damn'd and black
As hell, whereto it goes . . . '[62]

While later Christian preachers dwelt lovingly on detailed descriptions of the fate that awaited the souls of the damned in hell, the New Testament is fairly reticent on the subject. The only passage that offers anything like a description of the afterlife is found in the Gospel of Luke, and there is a dispute over its authenticity: it is the legend of the poor beggar Lazarus and the rich man, at whose gate he lay begging for bread. Folk tales about a poor man and a rich man whose fates are reversed in the next world are widely known in the ancient Near East.[63] Intriguingly, there is no mention of the rich man being punished for his sins, only for his wealth, which does sound like an authentic echo of Jesus, who warned that it would be easier for a camel to go through the eye of a needle, than for a rich man to enter the kingdom of God,[64] a text that seems to

have been quietly forgotten by the rich television evan-
gelists of the Christian Right.

> There was a certain rich man, which was clothed in
> purple and fine linen, and fared sumptuously every day:
> And there was a certain beggar named Lazarus, which
> was laid at his gate, full of sores, And desiring to be fed
> with the crumbs which fell from the rich man's table:
> moreover the dogs came and licked his sores. And it
> came to pass, that the beggar died, and was carried by
> the angels into Abraham's bosom: the rich man also died,
> and was buried; And in hell he lift up his eyes, being in
> torments, and seeth Abraham afar off, and Lazarus in his
> bosom. And he cried and said, Father Abraham, have
> mercy on me, and send Lazarus, that he may dip the tip
> of his finger in water, and cool my tongue; for I am
> tormented in this flame. But Abraham said, Son,
> remember that thou in thy lifetime receivedst thy good
> things, and likewise Lazarus evil things: but now he is
> comforted, and thou art tormented. And beside all this,
> between us and you there is a great gulf fixed: so that
> they who would pass from hence to you cannot; neither
> can they pass to us, that would come from thence.[65]

By the time we get to the Quran, hell and heaven are
being described in startling detail.

> After this sort will we recompense the transgressors.
> They shall make their bed in Hell, and above them
>   shall be coverings of fire . . .
> And the inmates of the fire shall cry to the inmates
>   of Paradise: 'Pour upon us some water!' . . .
>
> Oh! how wretched shall be the people of the
>   left hand!

Amid pestilential winds and in scalding water,
And in the shadow of a black smoke,
Not cool, and horrid to behold . . .
Then ye, O ye the erring, the gainsaying,
Shall surely eat of the tree Ez-Zakkoum . . .

It is a tree which cometh up from the bottom of hell;
Its fruit is as it were heads of Satans;
And, lo! the damned shall surely eat of it and fill
    their bellies with it:
Then shall they have, thereon, a mixture of boiling
    water . . .

Verily the tree of Ez-Zakkoum
Shall be the sinner's food:
Like dregs of oil shall it boil up in their bellies,
Like the boiling of scalding water.
'– Seize ye him, and drag him into the mid-fire;
Then pour on his head of the tormenting boiling
    water.
'– Taste this: for thou forsooth art the mighty, the
    honourable!
Lo! this is that of which ye doubted!'
But the pious shall be in a secure place,
Amid gardens and fountains,
Clothed in silk and richest robes, facing one
    another . . .

On inwrought couches
Reclining on them face to face:
Aye-blooming youths go round about to them
With goblets and ewers and a cup of flowing wine;
Their brows ache not from it, nor fails the sense:
And with such fruits as shall please them best,
And with flesh of such birds as they shall long for:

And theirs shall be the Houris, with large dark eyes,
   like pearls hidden in their shells,
In recompense for their labours past.[66]

The confident and conflicting intricacy of some of these descriptions of the soul should alert us to the uncertainty of it all. Of course, sceptical materialists will waste no time on any of these speculations, anyway. For them 'soul' is just another way of talking about the human mind, which is a function of the brain, a complex organ we know much more about than our forebears did when they embarked on their theories. Neuroscientists now divide the mind into discrete components of the brain and demonstrate how damage to these areas affects specific functions. Whether some core essence of the self stays alive and aware beneath the death or partial death of the brain is by no means clear. Recent accounts of people who have recovered from deep comas and, while unable to communicate, claim to have been aware of what was going on around them, suggest that there may be mysteries to the self neuroscience has not yet been able to fathom. Nevertheless, for materialists, the brain is to the mind what computer hardware is to computer software: without the former the latter is useless. Whatever analogies materialists offer to capture the experience of the elusive self, they do not believe it has any existence apart from its physical envelope. Consciousness may still be a bit of a mystery; the existence of the thinking, self-transcending human mind may be a bigger one; nevertheless, materialists believe that they are functions of the brain and they will go when it goes, die when it dies.

There is no ghost in the machine, no soul in the body. In us nature has certainly animated itself, but something even more momentous has happened. It is our privilege or our tragedy to have started thinking and thereby to have achieved some autonomy over nature. In fact, we have grown apart from our parent. It is this experience of the self's autonomy – its 'I'-ness – that makes it almost impossible not to speculate about the mystery of its nature and destiny. Like the robots who achieved feeling and consciousness in Ridley Scott's cult film *Blade Runner*, it is hard not to think – whatever the engineers say about us – there is more to us than animated chemistry. You *could* describe Elgar's Cello Concerto as the rubbing of horsehair over catgut, but while that description would be accurate as far as it went, you'd lose its essence, its soul. This is why, although they do not dispute the chemical account, some people persist in believing that functional materialism, while cogent and persuasive in so many ways, seems to be missing something.

The fact that we are engaged in this debate about *ourselves* at all, the fact that we are capable of promoting ourselves to eternity, even theoretically, shows just how extraordinary – and how dangerous – we are. It could even be argued that the invention of the human soul was the worst thing that could have happened to the other creatures with whom we share the earth. John Berger certainly thinks this is why animals have disappeared from our lives during the last two centuries.

The decisive theoretical break came with Descartes. Descartes internalised, *within man*, the dualism implicit in the human relation to animals. In dividing absolutely body from soul, he bequeathed the body to the laws of physics and mechanics, and, since animals were soul-less, the animal was reduced to the model of the machine . . . Eventually Descartes' model was surpassed. In the first stages of the industrial revolution, animals were used as machines . . . Later, in the so-called post-industrial societies, they are treated as raw material. Animals required for food are processed like manufac-tured commodities. [67]

Whether our ruthless domination of the other animals, which we discussed in the previous chapter, is the result of the way we have spiritualised ourselves, so that we now see our relationship with the earth not that of a passing guest, but that of owner and master, is certainly arguable. The other dangerous consequence of soul-thinking is its toxic influence on religious fanaticism of the suicide-bomber variety, not to mention the centuries of abuse that revolved round capturing and saving souls for eternity through religious missions. If we were more modest in our spiritual claims and saw 'soul', without the definite or indefinite article, as a temporal gift of nature rather than as an eternal entity, then we might start to enjoy it for its own sake, the way we enjoy a holiday in a friend's cottage, or a book we've borrowed from the library, without expecting either to last for ever. It is true that the idea of the immortal soul made in God's image contributed to the development of the idea of inalienable human rights – expressed in Kant's categorical imperative always to see others as ends and never as means or objects – and we should be grateful for that; but we can accept a good idea for its own sake without necessarily buying exaggerated claims about its origin. It is a good and fruitful idea to treat every human as a unique and priceless being, even if we can't accept the idea that they also possess immortal souls. Why can't we reverence and respect them for their own sake, as we ourselves like to be treated with respect? A simple ethic based on gratitude for the gift of life and respect for other creatures so gifted is both modest and practical. It might also serve to limit our tendency to moral inflation and the arrogance that usually goes with it.

The range of views on the mystery of human identity suggests that there could be something for everyone here, depending on the position, or hunch, from which we set out. The early myth of animated dust returning to its animator at death clearly carries usable meaning today. We could say that at death the organic returns to the inorganic state it came from, so in a sense nothing is lost and life goes on. If we are attracted to the idea of the earth as a living organism which gave birth to us, then we could see death as a necessity that is encompassed within the larger life of the planet, much as the body sheds cells throughout its period of existence. If we are drawn to some of the vaguer versions of theism and the possibility that some kind of intelligence infuses the universe, then we might be helped by the metaphor of death as a stream emptying into a river that empties into the living sea. True sceptics will spurn all these attempts to soften the reality of the absoluteness of death, and will gird themselves to endure their entry into oblivion with as much grace as they can muster.

Likewise, traditional believers will reject any attempt to dilute the idea of the immortality of the soul, and will continue to hope for the life of the world to come after death – provided they are confident of getting to their preferred destination on the other side.

Speaking personally, I find absolute assertions about the nature and destiny of the human soul increasingly hard to accept. So many trillions of trillions of those who have died since we got our souls – doing what? I don't much mind the Hollywood version of the after-life, meeting Audrey Hepburn under a tree and being guided into what looks like a lovely garden in perfect Californian weather, but even that is bound to pall in time: time being, of course, what we would have a horrifyingly endless supply of. And no animals! I wouldn't like that, especially if heaven is meant to be a reward for having had a hard time down here, considering what a tough time we've given the animals: we enslave them, abuse them, eat them – and zilch! If heaven is about justice it is going to be heaving with turkeys, chickens, pigs, sheep and cattle, not to mention all those miserable farmed salmon. No, it doesn't compute. Anyway, if animals don't have souls, as Descartes confidently asserted, yet we came from a previous state of animal development, at what point in evolution did *we* acquire them? Did we acquire them gradually, the way we acquired physical characteristics, or did we have to wait till a particular stage in human development before they were implanted? The more I think about it, the less I like the idea of *possessing* a soul. If I have to make a supernatural choice I'll go for the Hebrew idea: not a soul in a body, a ghost in a machine, but an animated whole: a thinking feeling yearning puzzling body with *soul*, the X factor, the bit that sings and prays and reaches out to others. And I've an idea that all that thinking feeling puzzling will go when I go. I hope so. I don't like crowds, and heaven must be getting increasingly crowded as every second people die on earth.

But what about the other place? I'm told the company is better, but if God loves animals it will be full of supermarket tycoons and factory farmers, a heartless bunch, so I'll pass on that too. It is the endless velvet night for me, thank you. Nevertheless, I would not want to persuade anyone out of belief in heaven, especially if it comforts them for a rotten life or consoles them for the death of a loved one. For all the confusions and inconsistencies of thinking about life after death, there is a logic to it that allows some sort of conformity with what we now know of nature and its processes. While the language of the myth of Creation is highly concrete, it is consistent with what we know was a process of gradual animation, from primordial life-forms to the full self-consciousness of the human. Super-Naturalists choose to believe that the agent of this process – the cause of things – was 'God'. Straight-Naturalists choose to believe that Nature, through some process we do not yet fully understand, popped into inorganic existence and later animated itself. Both the Super-Naturalist and Straight-Naturalist solutions to the puzzle of life share some characteristics. Each involves positing a self-existent reality, whether God or Nature, which we cannot get beyond, since there is no view from nowhere that affords us an objective, external perspective on the matter. But some minds refuse to be barged into either way of foreclosing the puzzle of existence, which is why some of us think the most honest response to these mysteries is a kind of expect-ant agnosticism that is more comfortable with the cloudy glimmerings of myth than the diamond-sharp clarities of religion or science. Even so, the agnostic will admit that it is certainly theoretically possible that there is an Uncaused Cause beyond our knowing that corresponds to something like the traditional picture of God; just as it will admit that it is theoretically possible that the universe is self-existent, with no beyond or outside from which any external agency could have acted upon it. Tragically, neither of these competing approaches has proved able to rescue humanity from its addiction to death and enslavement. While the myths of the Hebrew Bible reflect the catastrophic effect our cruelty and discon-tent have had on the earth and the creatures with whom we share it, later theological developments in Christianity and Islam seem more like eschatological expressions of our cruelty than challenges to it. The visions of hell in both traditions bear a remarkable similarity to what we have been doing to the earth for centuries, and do with more insistent fury year by year.

But there is another spiritual tradition that may contain enough wisdom and compassion to provide us with the stimulus we need to deal with the horrors we are creating for ourselves. Just as the Hebrew Creation myth in Genesis is conformable with what we now know of the evolu-tion of life on earth, so some of the psychological insights of Buddhism are conformable with what we now know

about the incessant discontents of the human psyche. For
the Buddha, we are not immortal souls inhabiting mortal
bodies; we are finite beings tragically aware of our own
transient hungers who seem destined to go on repeating
our mistakes in life after life, far into the future. This
sounds like a secular version of the Hindu Law of Karma.
Karma, meaning 'deeds' or 'works', is the idea that the way
we live in this life fixes the kind of life we'll lead in future
existences. Our thoughts, words and deeds have ongoing
ethical consequences that determine our future lives. In
Hindu thought this is understood literally, as an endless
process of rebirth. The Buddha, who appeared to uphold
this ancient Indian belief, modified it so radically as to
render it unrecognisable; yet in doing so he gave it enduring
value and usefulness. He taught the truth of the doctrine
of rebirth, but without having to believe that any soul
passed from one existence to another. If there is no soul
to migrate into another existence, what is passed on? The
Buddha understood how our incessant discontent plunges
ahead of itself to mark the lives of those who follow us,
as well as those around us now. While we ourselves will
not pass on into other forms of existence, the way we
have lived will leave its mark, for good or ill, on the world
our children and our children's children will inherit. Just
as the world wears the smudge and stain of *our* forebears,
so will it long bear the marks of the wounds we have
inflicted upon it. The Buddha was deeply aware of the
accumulating sorrow and final unreality of the 'I'. But
while he saw no solution to the burden of suffering we
pass on from one existence to the next – other than the
practice of detachment – he did urge the practice of

restraint and compassion while we are on our own journey to dissolution. If we are equally revolted by the cruel eschatologies of organised religion and the callous hedonism of modern secularism, we can make our protest by following the way of compassion. We are all, for a time, bound on the wheel of existence, whirling in space, before being thrown off it into the darkness: so why can't we acknowledge our common finitude, our brief time in the sun, and live in a way that honours the existence not only of our fellow humans, but of the other creatures who share our common journey to the grave? Compassion won't rob the world of its tragic harshness, nor will it remove the sadness we discover at the heart of a universe marked by change and decay. But it can help to soften the cry of grief as we all pass under the immitigable tree into the mystery beyond.

A good place to begin this work of compassion is applying it to the way we *think*. In spite of our confident protestations and taking of sides, we never can be quite certain about who we are, where we came from and where we are going: yet it is from that very uncertainty that our religious and intellectual responses to life have developed. Rather than destroying ourselves over our disagreements, why can't we bring some modesty and kindness to the endless debate we have with ourselves about ourselves? That, anyway, is what I shall try to reach for in the next chapter.

4
SUFFERING

Have you not heard of that madman who lit a lantern in the bright morning hours, ran to the market place, and cried incessantly: 'I seek God! I seek God!' — As many of those who did not believe in God were standing around just then, he provoked much laughter. Has he got lost? asked one. Did he lose his way like a child? asked another. Or is he in hiding? Is he afraid of us? Has he gone on a voyage? emigrated? — Thus they yelled and laughed.

NIETZSCHE

Anyone who has lost one they love to death is astonished that the world outside goes on about its business when their world has just ended. In the previous chapter I mentioned the disorienting effect my mother's death had on me. She died in the summer, and I can remember sitting dazed in the hot train as it carried me to see her body for the last time. The train trundled to a stop at stations on its accustomed route; some people got off and some people got on. The countryside I gazed at was languid in the heat, and under the trees cows flicked their tails to drive away persistent flies. Everything went on as usual around me, yet for me everything was changed. Strangely enough, only a few weeks before this I had preached about the problem of suffering to my Edinburgh congregation and had quoted W.H. Auden:

> About suffering they were never wrong,
> The Old Masters: how well, they understood
> Its human position; how it takes place
> While someone else is eating or opening a
>   window or just walking dully along;[68]

I hadn't then known another Auden poem that was to be made famous twenty years later by the Richard Curtis, Mike Newell film, *Four Weddings and a Funeral*. The most moving scene in the film was when Matthew, played by John Hannah, recited the poem at the funeral of his partner Gareth, exuberantly played by Simon Callow. The poem tells us that since this death even the stars are not wanted now, and that we can

> Pour away the ocean and sweep up the wood;
> For nothing now can ever come to any good. [69]

Suffering contracts everything into a timeless instancy. It also forces the great question from us about what it all means. That is why it is such a pity that we compound our troubles by disputing so violently with each other about their meaning. In its multitudinous forms, religion has supplied most of the answers to the question posed by suffering. The paradox is that its inherent disputatiousness adds greatly to the problem it so confidently sets out to solve for us. This is why many thinkers today not only reject it, they accuse it of being the source of most of the evils that afflict humankind. There is a particularly ugly debate going on about all this at the moment, which is why I think we should bring more modesty and kindness to the debate. I detect four kinds of response to the question life and its suffering puts before humanity. As with anything as uncertain and speculative as this, the responses lean into each other along a continuum, and an almost infinite number of shadings and variations are possible in capturing every nuance. Nevertheless, it is probably more helpful to define the types with some sort of precision and clarity, while remembering that nothing human is as neat as this is going to sound. The word that hovers above this whole area of concern is *meaning*. We normally reckon that for something to mean something there has to be someone to mean it, so the number one question is whether there is a knowable reality external to the universe that means it. The classic, pre-modern answer to the question was that the great meaner was God. In those days it stood to reason that, since nothing comes from nothing, nature had to have a meaner as well as a maker. Madness lay in trying to figure out who made the maker so, in order to stop the madness, the maker was defined as being himself unmade: he was self-existent and without beginning or end. That is what 'God' meant. Since I am bored with the debate that surrounds this question, and since I do not think it goes anywhere except in circles, I am not interested in saying who is right and who is wrong in the way it is still being argued about; though I am interested in trying to describe what people *think* about the issue. I'd rather say: this is how people actually think about these matters; than say: this is how people ought to think about these matters. At any rate, the former approach is what I want to attempt, but I need to enter another preliminary idea before diving into the vortex.

To explain it I want to use the metaphor of the radio signal. Before digital radio made everything crystal clear, many of us spent a lot of time in our cars twiddling with knobs to get the best signal from the broadcaster as we drove the length of the country. We were all familiar with the frustration of losing the signal completely as we drove through a mountain glen and picking it up again as we got into a large city. Behind the idea of God lies the related idea of *revelation*, which is itself a kind of radio broadcast. Back in the mists of time when humanity was believed to have been more psychically tuned to the divine frequency, God was understood to have announced himself to his creatures by a variety of revelatory devices, including visions, auditions, dreams and inspirations. Since the distant days of the clear signal there has been an interesting development. The divine broadcaster is no longer thought to speak directly to private individuals. The men in authority who always take charge of a religion once it has established itself are suspicious of people who claim to hear the divine voice; the kind of people, in fact, who get religions going in the first place. A bishop said to one who heard such voices, 'Sir, the pretending to extraordinary revelations and gifts of the Holy Ghost is a horrid thing, a very horrid thing.'[70] That is why the leaders who take over a faith always close down the community radio network and replace it with an officially

authorised written minute of the divine encounter with
the original listeners. They shut down the station and
replace it with a book, a visible text that can be made
publicly audible by recitation. The main advantage of this
is that it gives the leaders more control over their followers
than would have been possible had they all been allowed
to tune in directly to the voice of God. The official theory
was that there had once been a time when God spoke
directly to individuals, but that time was over. The line
had been disconnected for centuries, but this was not a
problem. During the period when God had been online
he had issued directions concerning all that humanity
needed to understand and order its life. These directions
had been saved for subsequent generations, so all they
had to do was open the file that contained the original
transactions, read it, and obey. The danger here is that,
now that they can read the original broadcasts for themselves, why do they need leaders to tell them what it
means? They have everything in writing now, and the
great thing about words on a page is that you can argue
endlessly about what they actually mean, in spite of official attempts to establish a single authorised meaning.
Books are notoriously subject to different interpretations.
That is why, in addition to the holy books themselves,
over the centuries other volumes have accrued round
them, offering us a variety of approaches to the meaning
of the original broadcasts. As is the way with these things,
these secondary texts achieved a hallowed reputation for
themselves and became subject, in their turn, to interpretation. This constantly ramifying process gave rise to
a vast scholarly industry called theology, whose methods,

to this day, are marked by extraordinary competitiveness and discord – which is probably not surprising, given the elusiveness of the subject of the study. From within this welter of claim and counter-claim I can detect four responses to the human quest for meaning.

Using the radio metaphor, I describe the first notch on this long continuum or spectrum as *strong* religion, because it claims to be in possession of a clear and perfect signal from the divine. Of course, we may hold that no human enterprise is impervious to change and the challenge of new knowledge, including religion; nevertheless, believers in strong religion are determined to keep their faith insulated from the eroding tides of history, if only in their own communities. There are too many examples of the phenomenon to make it possible to be at all inclusive in describing it, but a few symbolic examples will help to capture the flavour. Strong religions are both information and social systems: they claim to be owners of a body of revealed knowledge about how the universe came to be; and they claim to be in possession of the final and unalterable lifestyle manual, itself dictated by God during the original broadcasts. These claims inevitably put strong religion on a collision course with humanity's experience of history, which brings the constant challenge of new knowledge and new ways of living. An obviously current example is the dissonance between the Creationist account of the formation of the earth and its animal populations, and the received scientific account that is broadly accepted by educated secular opinion today. It is unnecessary to rehearse this already over-described phenomenon, but the essence of it is the commitment of the believer in strong religion to the inerrancy of ancient religious texts, such as the Bible. The views of the Bible, including its astronomy, are held to override all subsequent discoveries and the thinking that flows from them. If the Bible says God created the world and its inhabitants in six days, then that's that. The fact that some Creationists try to use science to support the biblical claim only goes to show that even they sometimes miss their own point, which is the absolute authority of the Bible and the need to commit totally to its opinions, even when they fly in the face of otherwise generally accepted knowledge. I knew a geneticist, a believing Christian, who tried to prove that parthenogenesis or virgin birth was scientifically possible. It did not seem convincing to me, but I thought his argument was beside the point anyway: the significance of a virgin birth is not its provable conformity with nature, but its miraculous character: with God all things are possible, even things that go directly against the laws of nature. This is the pure faith position, and it actually gathers strength from what the world deems to be its absurdity, which is why the apostles of secularity are wasting their time trying to challenge its adherents on the grounds of reason. The puniness of human reason and its proud discoveries are held to be nothing compared to the power of Almighty God.

The other side of this counter-cultural defiance relates to social systems. Not only is the knowledge or science of thousands of years ago held to be permanently definitive, so are the social arrangements, such as the status of women or gay people. The most dramatic symbol of

strong religious resistance to contemporary norms is the
recent appearance on the streets of European cities of
Muslim women covered completely in the *burqa*, an
enveloping outer garment that cloaks the entire body.
The fact that the *burqa* is not mentioned in the Qur'an,
and that its use is interpreted in different ways by Islamic
scholars, is irrelevant to the point here. The dramatic
otherness of the sight of a woman enveloped in a *burqa*,
shopping in a British supermarket, is a sign of religious
anxiety as well as defiance. It is an eloquent challenge to
the objectifying force of the hot gaze of male sexuality;
yet its very protectiveness towards women is itself an
objectifying force. We could say, therefore, that the attempt
of a school board in Kansas to require the teaching of
Creationism in local schools and the decision of Muslim
women in Bradford to start wearing the *burqa* are both
symbols of the counter-cultural assertion of the strong
religious position. And noting an interesting distinction
might make the defiance clearer here. In settled religious
cultures, tradition*al* believers usually take their ritual practices and convictions unselfconsciously for granted as the
way things are, without having to think much about
them. By contrast, the traditional*ist* believer, perhaps living
in a plural secular culture, is one who defiantly and very
self-consciously chooses to act in ways that run counter
to prevailing norms. *Traditionalism* is a perspective that is
closer to ideology than to faith, in the sense that it is a
worked-out set of ideas that defines itself in self-conscious
opposition to other systems. The clue to the presence of
the ideological mindset is the presence of the tell-tale
little suffix -ism. Creationism, fundamentalism, Marxism,

global market capitalism are all distinguished by an inter-
locking set of ideas which add up to a total system that
has to be applied in an undeviatingly formulaic way. This
strongly ideological use of religion is prevalent in our
world today. Commentators note many inconsistencies
in the strong religious position, the main one being the
way it skilfully uses the technologies of modernity to
challenge modernity. For example, Islamist movements
that call for the establishment of a universal caliphate are
brilliant at using the internet and mobile phone networks
– the iconic devices of modernity – to undermine the
very system that makes their campaigning so effective.
And no Christian Evangelist in the USA could hold his
own against the competition without his sophisticated
digital broadcasting network.

Yet for all their confidence that there is no question
their faith cannot answer, the existence of suffering poses
the most taxing philosophical difficulty for strong believers
– or, if not for the believers themselves, certainly for those
who study the claims they make. The problem lies with
the very meaning of 'God'. By definition, God has to be
identified in superlatives. Humans may possess some
knowledge, but God possesses all knowledge. Humans
may possess some power, but God possesses all power.
Humans may possess some goodness, but God possesses
all goodness. The logic in all of this is clear enough.
Humans have what philosophers call a contingent existence: God, not themselves, is the source of their being;
so their attributes and capacities depend on their source
or creator. We have already tried to think about the
impossibility of getting back to before the Big Bang, back

to what was there before there was any there *there*. As we have seen, scientists fill that gap by postulating what they call a singularity, an unknown mystery that stands in for what our knowledge cannot yet explain. In a sense, God is a philosophical singularity, a way of filling the abyss that yawns at the beginning of the causal sequence. And just as the scientific singularity has to contain in embryonic form the whole of the expanding universe; so God has to be the source not only of the material, but of the moral and spiritual universe, the universe of values. Each singularity has to contain all subsequent history in germ, which is where the divine singularity hits its greatest difficulty. It does not make sense to hold the scientific singularity morally responsible for subsequent history, because it is not thought to be a responsible agent capable of intention: it is best characterised as blind force. Even the scientific myth is not without its problems, of course, because it still leaves us with the difficulty of explaining the emergence of pity in an indifferent universe. The divine singularity faces the opposite problem. By definition it is held to be not the blind, but the intentional source of all things, including morality. It is the fount of all virtue, the source of all meaning. There are some physical analogies that capture the moral neutrality or indifference of the scientific singularity: we could liken it to an impersonal surge of electricity, for instance. But all the analogies for the divine singularity ultimately ground themselves in some idea of personal responsibility. It would be odd to hold the scientific singularity morally responsible for the Holocaust, because it has no personal will. But if God is God as defined in the Western tradition, possessing will and intention and in some superabundant sense being a *person*, then the buck has to stop with him: ultimately he is responsible for the Holocaust and for everything else. How do strong believers respond to this colossal challenge?

Not very convincingly, it has to be said. In the Christian tradition the problem of suffering has a whole theological department to itself called 'theodicy', from the Greek words for god and justice. This aspect of theological scholarship sets out to defend God from the charge of being complicit in or responsible for the cruelty of his universe. But that way of putting the problem already suggests a development in thinking about God. To the early superstitious mind the issue was not to explain divine cruelty, but to avoid it. Primitive religion takes it for granted that the gods are capricious monsters, who can sometimes be bought off, like all bullies, by bribes or distractions. The sacrifice system probably had its origins here. From the beginning humans have always found it hard to get their heads round God, to figure out what he is like in himself, so they had to fall back on analogies with the human. For the primitive mind it stood to reason that if God is ultimate power, *the* X force, then the closest likeness to him on earth is the tyrant or absolute ruler. And since you never knew when, like Al Capone, he was going to take a baseball bat to your skull, experience taught that it was wise to keep the big man sweet and walk warily in his presence.

The arbitrariness of this omnipotent sadism evolved

into something more systematic in the first theory of suffering, which was premised on the discovery that, contrary to earlier understandings of the divine, God actually had ethics. Suffering was then believed to be punishment for sin, for offending God's righteousness. There is clearly a moral logic in thinking that offenders should be brought to book for their misdeeds, and it lies behind the evolution of all systems of criminal justice. How precisely God engages with the justice system has been endlessly speculated upon to little coherent effect. The most consistent theory is the idea of the final judgement, whether immediately after death or at some grand reckoning thereafter, when the books will be opened and we will be called to account for what we have done during our sojourn on earth. Apart from the dramatic symmetry of the idea, it is theoretically calculated upon a precise record of all our doings, presumably gathered through the agency of some kind of infallible surveillance system. But the final judgement solution to the problem of suffering provoked by human evil was not the earliest one on offer: there was also a continuous-assessment-and-immediate-judgement theory, but it has had a chequered history. The theory was that the universe was rigged with CCTV cameras that noted offending behaviour and instantly punished it. You could tell who had broken the code by their sufferings. Since God rewarded the righteous and punished the wicked, if you were doing well you were held to be righteous, and if you were doing badly you were held to be vicious. Its most eloquent expression is found in Psalm 37:

Fret not thyself because of evildoers, neither be thou envious against the workers of iniquity. For they shall soon be cut down like the grass, and wither as the green herb . . . For evildoers shall be cut off: but those that wait upon the Lord, they shall inherit the earth. For yet a little while, and the wicked shall not be: yea, thou shalt diligently consider his place, and it shall not be.

Intriguingly, the most interesting book in the Hebrew Bible is a precisely targeted reply to this theory of human suffering. The Book of Job tackles the theory head-on. Job, a righteous man – and known by God to be righteous – is subjected to horrendous suffering in order to test his trust in God. The reader, having read the prologue to the book where the test is approved, knows what is going on, but Job's conventionally minded friends are not in on the conspiracy. Having witnessed the onslaught of suffering that has engulfed their friend, they gather round him not to bring comfort, but to interrogate him on the basis of their unthinking acceptance of the official theory: what have you been up to, Job, that God has sent such punishment upon you? Job, on the other hand, has been asking *God* a question based on the same theory: you know that I am righteous, yet here I am, suffering unbelievable torments, so what is going on, what has happened to the competence of your system? While the book answers the question put *to* Job by his so-called comforters, it never really answers the question put *by* Job to God. God wipes the floor with Job's friends for their slavish adherence to the official theory, but while he pronounces Job innocent, he never really offers a justification for his sufferings. All he does is pull rank on him and bluster like an offended prelate: 'Shall he that contendeth with the Almighty instruct him?'[71]

This ancient theory is so easy to falsify from the most cursory examination of history that it is a surprise to find it still actively propounded as a way of explaining the sufferings that beset humanity, but it hangs around the human psyche like an old guilt, probably because it is ingrained in the collective consciousness of the race. Anyone who has engaged in pastoral work will recognise its enduring residue in the cry: 'What have I done to deserve this? I try to lead a good life, then this happens . . . ' And it operates at the collective as well as the personal level: God, apparently, not only punishes individuals for their offences, he punishes whole societies for the misdeeds of individuals. We heard this response from the late Jerry Falwell, a leader of strong Christian fundamentalism in the US, who claimed that the atrocity of 9/11 was God's punishment on liberal America for its support of abortion and gay rights. A similar accusation was heard from Muslim clerics in Indonesia after the tsunami on Boxing Day 2004: Allah was cleansing the land of the corrupting effects of Western tourism on their previously pure Islamic society. A variant of the theory was heard during the early years of the AIDS pandemic, when evangelical clerics pronounced it God's judgement on homosexuals. It was 'the gay plague', and the echo of the plagues with which God smote the Egyptians was intentional not accidental. No one seemed bothered that a God who was capable of designing a virus precisely targeted against sexual misconduct was uninterested in targeting arms manufacturers

or international drug cartels with the same sophisticated precision.

In thinking about God's responsibility for suffering,
theologians make a distinction between suffering caused
by natural forces and suffering caused by intentional
human acts such as 9/11. We have already noticed how
we are caught between the monster and the saint in the
human struggle; between those who serve and those who
destroy human community. We have noticed how easy
it is for us to stand by and permit evil to prosper. And
we have observed how we often collude with the great
destroyers of joy in the human community. Theologians
have suggested that this lets God off one of the hooks
of suffering. He has given us freedom of will, so we, not
he, are clearly responsible for the use we make of it. If
I give you a high-powered motorcycle and you plough
it into a bunch of schoolchildren it is your fault, not
mine, for the death and maiming that ensue. Well, up to
a point. On the other hand, if you, being all-knowing,
were well aware of how careless I was likely to be with
such a dangerous piece of machinery, then surely you
bear some responsibility for what has happened? Anyway,
it is not as though freedom of will has been handed out
to humanity, complete with information-counselling and
health warnings. We have already seen how messy and
confused our human consciousness is, and how partial
and emergent our grasp of freedom is. Nevertheless,
theologians are expert at utilising unlikely material to
support their cause, and the difficulty we all find in
learning to live responsibly is cited in evidence here.
There is no doubt that much of the suffering that has

afflicted the human community in the last hundred years
– to go back no further – has been caused by human
agency. Between them, three of the great monsters of the
twentieth century – Hitler, Stalin and Mao Tse-Tung –
were responsible for the deaths and incalculable suffering
of hundreds of millions. Nevertheless, while this distinction may be a commendable example of theological
improvisation, the attempt to limit God's responsibility
for suffering to natural disasters still leaves him with a
pretty long charge-sheet, unless we can smuggle in some
idea of cosmic responsibility and start blaming nature
itself. Actually, Saint Paul seemed to believe that the planet
was the victim of some sort of moral catastrophe that
wrested it from the peace of Eden to a situation he
likened to a woman in a long and painful labour. But
however we slice it, it remains difficult for many people
to square what they know about life on earth with any
idea of a beneficent creator. We know that animal life is
essentially a food chain, characterised by the species
preying on each other. As a consequence, suffering, fear
and distress are intrinsic, not incidental, to its processes.
It may be that if animals lack imagination and foresight
their suffering is limited to the spasm of the chase and
the kill; whereas humans, because of their consciousness,
die many deaths in anticipation of the one that finally
gets them; and make their lives a kind of misery by the
psychological sufferings to which they are prone. That is
why attempts to exonerate God from responsibility for
suffering have been least emotionally successful when
they have been articulated with the greatest calculation.
If there is such a supernatural being, endowed with the

attributes we have bestowed upon him, why didn't he see all this coming and pull the plug on the experiment and start again? Better still, why not stay out of the creation business entirely and settle for his own presumably perfect existence? Thousands of volumes have been written on this subject, and the fact that they go on being written shows that there is no likely end in sight to the compulsive theorising that dogs the issue. But it has to be said that strong believers are not deterred by the noisy contention that surrounds this debate. For them, all questions will one day be answered by the God in whom they implicitly trust. And one of the most enduring paradoxes of the situation is that strong religious faith is undoubtedly one of the most potent resources on earth for sustaining humans in the face of the torments of existence. For many, that is argument enough.

If strong religion deservedly gets most of the headlines today, the next notch on my typological continuum provokes the most undeserved contempt. Reverting to the radio signal metaphor, we could describe the people who occupy this place as those who receive a weak and intermittent signal from God. However, it would be a mistake to force the metaphor too literally here. It is not that *weak* religionists, unlike their strong counterparts, happen to possess poor equipment and are therefore unable to pick up the messages of the divine broadcaster. It is that they believe all human receivers to be so intrinsically flawed as to be incapable of interpreting the divine signals with any kind of reliable clarity, so they stamp all their recordings with the seal of uncertainty and provisionality. While they do not necessarily doubt the existence of the divine meaner, they are absolutely certain about the nature of the human confuser, and they have learnt not to put too much confidence in his claims. Humans can never be sure of the meaning behind the signals of transcendence they receive, because they themselves are the faulty equipment that has to interpret them, and history shows how fatally inadequate they have been at the game. Much blood has been spilt over rival interpretations of these elusive signals, and much human unhappiness has been engendered by the violent disagreements they have provoked. That is why the practitioners of weak religion try to inculcate theological modesty. They say to us: there is a tremendous mystery here and, while it fascinates us, there is so little we can certainly say about it that it behoves us to speak sparingly of it and deal graciously with one another when we share our own feeble interpretations of it.

Another element that differentiates the weak from the strong believer is in their attitudes to human society. Weak religion does not set itself on a collision course with the culture in which it is set, but allows itself to be influenced and modified by it; just as it, in turn, seeks to influence the surrounding culture with its own insights and discoveries. This is because it sees itself as an integral part of the community of the present as well as of the past. While it reverences and learns from the religious tradition that has nurtured it, it also respects the society of its own time and learns to go on adapting to its best discoveries. Psychoanalysts make an interesting distinction in the use of the word 'adapt'. If I have difficult parents, as a child I may learn to adapt myself to their arbitrary and bizarre behaviour. My character has been adapted to the context they have set for me, much as I might adapt to life inside, were I ever imprisoned. But though I have adjusted to the circumstances, I am not really free: I am constrained by forces I have learnt to deal with but have no real control over. Adaptive behaviour is different. The free person, secure in her own nature, is able to respond with improvisational skill to the events and circumstances that life brings her. Weak religion is adaptive in this sense. It is secure enough in its own values not to be thrown by the discoveries of the culture of which it is part. An example of the improvisational skill of weak religion is the way it adopted the scientific study of history in order to interrogate its own sacred texts, leading to an enormous scholarly industry in the study of the Bible and a radical re-interpretation of many of its claims. Just as important was its attempt to adapt to the human-relations revolutions of the modern era, in particular to the emancipation of women and the liberation of gay and lesbian people. This is ongoing business, of course, and homosexuality, in particular, is the subject of an intense struggle in the Anglican Communion, a body that is an uncomfortable mix of strong and weak believers.

I have already referred to the contempt in which weak religionists are held, not only by their strong counterparts, but by many who totally reject religion as baseless and irrational. Obviously, if you reject religion because you believe it to be irrational and non-adaptive, you will want it to fit your definition. You will prefer it to be obscurantist, misogynistic, homophobic, illiberal and contemptuous of modernity. Where it is trying to adapt itself to the best discoveries of humanity, while being true to the good values of its own tradition, it is likely to upset your one-dimensional oppositional typology. Thinking about another target of the neo-atheist movement is instructive here. It is no accident that this movement is as contemptuous of the psychoanalytic movement as it is of religion; nor is it surprising that it dismisses Sigmund Freud as scornfully as it rejects the high priests of religion. What weak religion and psychotherapeutic practice have in common is that each, in essence, is a clinical art not an academic science; which is why, at their best, they are constantly adaptive to the complexity of human need. Each uses the power of myth to help men and women adjust to the pains of existence. Each is a work of the human imagination built up over years of listening to the needs of human beings. And each is premised not on making grand scientific claims about factual reality, but on helping people get by in a cruel universe. Paradoxically, it is the theoretical uncertainty of the practitioners of both clinical disciplines that is their strength. Neither offers a strong take-it-or-leave-it message to struggling human beings. Rather, by a persistent and deep listening to human need they have created a responsive almonry, an improvisational art or form of therapeutic jazz that is of actual use to people. Freud used Greek mythology to interpret the struggles of the human psyche. Much of what he came up with was fanciful, and most of it was unverifiable in any real scientific sense, but human beings found it helpful, because it gave them a way of understanding their own inner conflicts. Take, for example, his theory of the unconscious mind. We know our minds don't come in three detectable layers, like a car park, with the id in the basement, the superego on the second floor, and the ego between them on the first floor. But that way of describing the indescribable corresponds to the way we often feel about our inner struggles. Sometimes we are overwhelmed by inappropriate desires we find difficult to control; and we either let them overpower us, and pay the price of excess; or we overcorrect them, and pay the price of neurotic repression. This dilemma is as old as humanity. It is expressed in the ancient tension between the genial sensuality of Southern European Catholicism and the moral severity of Northern European Protestantism. The Polish journalist Ryszard Kapuściński says the same tension is at the very heart of Islam, and is physically expressed by the ancient city of Algiers, which is caught between the open Mediterranean current that looks to the sea, and the brooding fear of modernity found in desert Islam on the other side of the Atlas mountains.[12] But the tension is older than either Christianity or Islam. It is found in classical Greek thought, described by Nietzsche as the conflict between the Dionysian and the Apollonian, the ecstasy of the senses versus controlled rationality. Its most thrilling contemporary artistic expression is David Greig's version of Euripides' *The Bacchae*. Like the myth and drama of Ancient Greece, much of what Freud said about the battles of the soul corresponds to human experience; and who gives a damn whether it is 'true' or not: like adaptive religion, it helps us cope with life, and what is wrong with that? It is no accident that weak theology and clinical psychotherapy have developed alliances over the years, prompting a new discipline which actually calls itself 'clinical theology', which uses the myths and tropes of religion in a therapeutic way.

Unsurprisingly, weak religion has profoundly modified the traditional image of God, moving it away from the model of absolute power to one of responsive, suffering love. God is no longer envisaged as the irate ruler offended by his delinquent subjects, but as a grieving parent whose heart is broken by his erring children. This gentler understanding of God has had a profound effect on the way weak religion responds to the problem of suffering; and it is one that carries immense emotional power: it is the concept of the suffering and dying God. It moves the argument away from theory about God towards a mystical identification with those who suffer, leading to practical action: the problem of suffering is now no longer about explaining it, but about responding to it. Talk ceases. Work starts. Wounds are bound. Bruised feet are bathed. Believers find God among the suffering. They live with the dying street people of Calcutta. They join the rejected of the earth in the *villas miseria* and *favelas* of Latin America, in the ghettos of North America and in places of despair and hopelessness throughout the world. God's long-awaited answer to Job turns out to be not a clinching argument that solves the problem of suffering: it is to become Job.

With the practice of active compassion there goes a new theology of a God who submits himself to the cruelties of the wicked. Sometimes this is described as an act

of self–limitation or 'kenosis', from the Greek for
emptying. In the Christian tradition, the crucifixion of
Jesus carries some of these ideas. Because it cannot bear
the revealing light of goodness, evil always has to reach
out and quench it. But God does not stand by: it is God
who is shamed, God who walks on broken feet to Calvary,
God who hangs, naked, from the tree. This is an ancient
heresy called 'patripassianism', heretical because it
contained the forbidden idea that God in his distant
majesty could feel the pains of his children and suffer
with them. Rediscovered by theologians who were
silenced by the horrors of the twentieth century, it is
more a prayer of longing than a precise doctrine. If there
is a god at all, it is felt, he has to be a suffering and
dying god, a god on a cross: no other god will do. But
if there is a moral case for a dying god, there is also a
philosophical case. If there is that which we mean by God
– the ultimate ground and source of all reality – then
we are as unlikely to be able to comprehend it as a
bacterium in the gut of an elephant could be expected
to describe its host. There is a long tradition in philosophical theology which claims we can never say what
God is, only what God is not; but because humans have
failed to understand that truth, their history is littered
with dead gods. The madman in Nietzsche's *The Gay
Science*, who lit a lantern in the bright morning hours
and ran to the market to proclaim the death of God to
the scoffing bystanders, realised he had come too early:
'My time is not yet. This tremendous event is still
on its way, still wandering; has not yet reached the
ears of men.'[73] It has reached them now. What remains

uncertain is whether it is only an idea we go on killing – or something infinitely more precious.

Before thinking about the other places on my continuum of meaning, I want to offer a concluding reflection on both strong and weak religion. Each is a system of thought and practice that responds to the mystery of existence. It would be fair to describe strong religion as a closed system. Though I do not necessarily offer that description as a criticism, there are a number of important consequences of adopting the strong position. The closed system tends to lock one into the mindset and social scheme of a previous era. Of course, there is no absolute reason why one should not make this choice, because it is far from obvious that *later* is necessarily *better* in evaluating human history. One might even decide to pick and mix the best bits of different epochs, admiring, for example, first-century sexual mores, while preferring twenty-first-century dentistry. The downside of the comprehensiveness of the strong system is that it closes its practitioners off from the best as well as the worst of contemporary values, some aspects of which I have already explored. If I have a particular objection to strong religion it is aimed less at its cognitive side – it does not really bother me if someone chooses to believe the world was fashioned by God in six days – than at the consequential cruelty of its social ethic. If you believe, as I do, that cruelty is the greatest vice, then you will have to oppose a creed that condemns gay people and subordinates women and, when it is in a position to do so, actively persecutes the former group and represses the latter.

Weak religion, on the other hand, though it also tries to be systematic in its thinking, is more open and porous to the context in which it is set, and is better at appropriating the best values of secular culture, while challenging the worst. We could say of it, therefore, that it tries to pick the best bits from the constant flux of history. The obvious advantage of strong religion is that it will do your thinking about ultimate issues for you, if that is what you want, and let you get on with the rest of your life; weak religion, on the other hand, will expect you to do a lot of the work yourself, even if you are ill-equipped for the task.

The third notch on my continuum lacks the systematic approach of organised religion, in either its strong or weak forms. Though it retains a positive attitude towards the enterprise, it does not accept religion's estimate of itself. I call this place *after-religion*, because it is represented by people who have either moved from the centre of religious theory towards the edge; or by people who have moved from indifference or hostility to a more sympathetic understanding of the phenomenon. People in this position see religion as an entirely human construct, a work of the human imagination, but one that carries enduring meaning. Even the ugly and unsympathetic side of religion is not without its value to them, because it says something about the struggles of humanity with its own complex nature. The religious imagination is childlike in its ability to dive into the dark side of the psyche, as well as into its enduring longing for peace and harmony. The novelist Alasdair Gray described God as the strongest character in world fiction. It follows that the study of God will provide us with a straight route into the divided heart of his maker. Freud dismissed God because he was a human projection. But why the haste? Why not study the projection to find out what it tells us about ourselves? People who are after-religion are able to do this. They may even go to synagogue, church or mosque – regularly or from time to time – because they want to stay in touch with one of the oldest and most enduring of human institutions. Just as importantly, they do not want to cut off themselves or their children from the old truth-bearing myths, the ancient metaphors, the vivid tropes and images. They want to go on dipping into this mighty river. For them religion is a great work of art, something made by the human imagination. They know there is no single way of responding to art, so they refuse to let themselves be disturbed by the noisy posturing of official priesthoods. Politely, they go their own way, keep their own souls. We might describe this as the aesthetics of after-religion, so it is important to remember that there is an ethical side to the position as well, particularly in its response to human suffering, and the atheist Richard Rorty expressed it with characteristic generosity. Rorty was an anti-theoretical theorist – and he was well aware of the irony – who described himself as a pragmatist. He agreed with Marx that the important thing is not to explain the world, but to change it, especially its cruelties and oppressions. Rorty probably preferred Marx's Communist Manifesto to the New Testament, but for him the important thing about them both was that they kept alive the hope that our future

might be better than our past and that human suffering might be alleviated.

> It would be best, of course, if we could find a new docu-
> ment to provide our children with inspiration and hope
> – one which was as free of the defects of the New
> Testament as of those of the Manifesto. It would be good
> to have a reformist text, one which lacked the apoca-
> lyptic character of both books – which did not say that
> all things must be made new, or that justice 'can be
> attained only by the forcible overthrow of all existing
> social conditions'. It would be well to have a document
> which spelled out the details of a this-worldly utopia
> without assuring us that this utopia will emerge full-
> blown, and quickly, as soon as some single decisive change
> has occurred – as soon as private property has been abol-
> ished, or as soon as we have all taken Jesus into our
> hearts.
>
>   It would be best, in short, if we could get along
> without prophecy and claims to knowledge of the forces
> which determine history – if generous hope could sustain
> itself without such reassurances. Some day perhaps we
> shall have a new text to give our children – one which
> abstains from prediction yet still expresses the same
> yearning for fraternity as does the New Testament, and
> is as filled with sharp-eyed descriptions of our most
> recent forms of inhumanity to each other as the
> Manifesto. But in the meantime we should be grateful
> for two texts which have helped make us better – have
> helped us overcome, to some degree, our brutish self-
> ishness and our cultivated sadism.[74]

It is possible to respect religion because, at its best, it
challenges our brutish selfishness and our cultivated
sadism, as well as offering us the hope of a better future

for the world and its children. The hope is never fully realised, of course, because we are caught for ever in the tension between the monster and the saint, but nor does it ever fully fade. Exposure to religion's best dreams is one of the most enduring ways of keeping generous hope alive.

The fourth place on the continuum is the complete absence of religious consciousness, and it comes in both strong and weak forms. It is a sort of counter-aesthetic, inasmuch as it is totally deaf or colour-blind to the imagination that conjures up the religious response to the mystery of life. It is totally uninterested in the possibility of the Other that so obsesses the rest of humanity, and just doesn't get it. Its most positive characteristic is its complete acceptance of life without neurotically needing some external meaning to make it bearable. Life is its own meaning. It just is. So get on with it. It does not correspond to anything except itself. Anyway, there is no other place from which to evaluate it, no place outside from which to view it overall. We can't get off what we are on in order to see what it looks like from somewhere else, any more than we can *be* someone else in order to find out how we come across to others. We are stuck where we are and with what we are. It is through our senses that we get in touch with what is outside ourselves, but they can only put us in touch with what is available to them; and, by definition, the hypothetical divine or supernatural realm is unavailable to sense perception – which is precisely why it is a hypothesis, not a verifiable reality. Those who occupy this place are, to their frequent bemusement, aware that many people choose to treat the heavenly hypothesis as real: they not only build castles in the air, they actually try to live in them. To *fourth notchers* of the weak form this is viewed either as an endearing eccentricity to be tolerated, or as an example of a comforting faith they wish they could achieve themselves in their own times of suffering. In either case their response is completely without hostility and may even be tinged with occasional regret.

Strong fourth notchers are a different breed, and in their evangelical intensity they bear a marked resemblance to the religious protagonists they most despise. Like strong religionists, they are not content to keep their own certainties to themselves, and insist on spreading them to others. Intriguingly, the main motive for their current attack on religion actually exposes the greatest weakness of their position. The most passionate neo-atheists are motivated by a strongly ethical and entirely praiseworthy loathing of cruelty and violence. As any unbiased observer will agree, religion has been a potent force for cruelty and violence, both in the past and in recent experience, so it is not surprising that some of its opponents see it as a unique stimulus to evil conduct. One commentator has gone so far as to say that while anyone can persuade evil people to do evil things, only religion can persuade *good* people to do evil things. It is the theory that religion is the root of all evil that lies at the heart of the new atheism, but it is a flawed thesis. The common factor in the cruelty that disfigures human history is humanity itself. As we have already noted, the human animal is the most murderous species on the planet, and almost anything can provide us with an occasion for violence, including religion: but so can politics, nationalism, race, sex, greed for land – even football. Religion has had a terrible record in stoking and provoking violence; but it has also had a noble record in withstanding it. It is true that religion can make bad people worse, but it can also make good people better: which is why it is unfair to condemn its monsters without acknowledging its saints. In spite of its bitter rejection by some of our ablest thinkers today, I shall argue in the final part of this book that it is the myths and metaphors of religion that provide us with some of the deepest insights into the human condition, and offer us the best hope of saving ourselves from ourselves. Nevertheless, strong fourth notchers have much to commend them, not least their hatred of cruelty and cant and the courageous stoicism they commend in the face of suffering. As with most of these things, we are more likely to be drawn to our position on the spectrum as much by temperament and circumstance as by carefully worked-out conviction. And if this brief survey of human attitudes to religion teaches anything, it is probably best summed up in the words with which Stephen Vincent Benét ended his great poem, *John Brown's Body*:

> If you at last must have a word to say,
> Say neither, in their way,
> 'It is a deadly magic and accursed,'
> Nor 'It is blest,' but only 'It is here.'[75]

III
PLAY TIME

5
COMEDY

Our interest's on the dangerous edge of things.
The honest thief, the tender murderer,
The superstitious atheist . . .

ROBERT BROWNING

It can be a mistake to meet an artist whose work one reveres. One of the many paradoxes of creative genius is that it often makes its abode in unattractive habitations. Brilliant actors provide the clearest example of this. Many actors are interesting human beings in their own right, but not all. Some of our greatest actors have been people so uncertain of their own identity that they only came alive on stage or screen, while inhabiting someone else's life. Without naming him, I am thinking of one of the most famous actors of our time, whose presence on the screen is electrifying, yet who is reduced to mumbling incoherence when interviewed about his own life or attitudes. This would have been no surprise to that great poet but not entirely attractive human being, W.H. Auden. Auden made a fundamental distinction between the artist and the art, the maker and the thing made. Something he said about W.B. Yeats captured what he meant:

> You were silly like us; your gift survived it all:
> The parish of rich women, physical decay,
> Yourself . . . [76]

Auden talked about the lack of relation 'between the moral quality of a maker's life and the aesthetic value of the works he makes'; 'Every artist knows that the sources of his art are what Yeats called "the foul rag-and-bone shop of the heart", its lusts, its hatreds, its envies.'[77] That is why Auden hated the idea of anyone writing his biography; but I suspect that, though proud of his work yet ashamed of his life, he understood the vital connection between the two. He knew that his art was its own thing, whatever its origins, and should not be compromised by association with its maker's lusts, hatreds and envies: nevertheless, it was through the particular chemistry of his own experience that his art was born. In spite of their protestations, this is why we continue to be fascinated by the private lives of great artists. We wonder at the miracle of the rose blooming on a dung heap, but we recognise the mysterious connection between the two. Yeats understood this instinctively, as Crazy Jane reminds us:

> A woman can be proud and stiff
> When on love intent;
> But Love has pitched his mansion in
> The Place of Excrement;
> For nothing can be sole or whole
> That has not been rent.[78]

The fact that a corrupt tree can bear good fruit is a truth religious traditions find it hard to accept, just as strong atheists find it difficult to admit that the corrupt tree of religion continues to bear beautiful fruit. The fact is that everything we have achieved of beauty or goodness has sprung from the harsh soil of nature. Darwin advised us to use our imaginations to capture a sense of the ruthlessness of the natural forces that lurk beneath the bright surface of things. Reflective religious thinkers are no strangers to the darkness that lurks beneath the surface of things, but they find it hard to admit that from the beginning religion's mansions have also been pitched in the place of excrement. It is this foundational act of denial that accounts for the concept of blasphemy, the conviction that the constitutive elements of religion, especially its sacred figures, should be exempted from the normal processes of criticism and parody. The very existence of the idea of blasphemy suggests that acute anxiety about its claims has been embedded in religion since the beginning. Like a social climber in denial about his lowly origins, religion refuses to admit its dodgy start in life. In the previous chapter I looked at the way believers in what I called strong religion claimed to be in touch with a divine power that transcended the universe yet sought contact with humankind; and I explored some responses to that ancient claim. But how did that idea emerge in the first place and how can we use it today? In this chapter I want to suggest that one way to understand religion is to see it as a product of the creative power of the human mind, a work of art. Like any other work of art, including great poetry, its dubious origins should not be allowed to undermine its enduring value. Seen in that light, religion can go on illuminating the human condition.

A good place to start is with a mysterious character called Abraham, of whom we catch glimpses through the mists that obscure the origins of Judaism, Christianity and Islam, the three faiths that think of themselves as Abrahamic religions. The Book of Genesis tells us that Abraham was the patriarch who begat Isaac, who begat Jacob, who begat the Twelve Tribes of Israel, who ended up as slaves in Egypt, whence Moses led them into history. However obscure Abraham was, and however uncertain the facts about him, the traditions about him bequeathed to the three religions which claim him as their ancestor an ancient practice that is baffling to the secular mind: he listened to a voice in his head to which he accorded absolute authority. It is worth looking at the story, because it tells us a lot about religion and why many people are increasingly uncomfortable with it. The text in question comes in Genesis, chapter 22:

> And it came to pass after these things, that God did tempt Abraham, and said unto him, Abraham: and he said, Behold, here I am. And he said, Take now thy son, thine only son Isaac, whom thou lovest, and get thee into the land of Moriah; and offer him there for a burnt offering upon one of the mountains which I will tell thee of.

Nowadays we would hospitalise someone who obeyed an order like that, but in Abraham's time it was probably an essential requirement for the founder of a religion. The origins of religion are as hazy as the origins of

Abraham himself, but one educated guess is that when self-consciousness started flickering into life in early humans and they started talking to themselves in their own heads, the way we all do, they assumed someone else was on the line. This gave rise to a binary or bifurcated view of reality, resulting in what historians of culture call the bicameral mind. The voice in the head that is an inescapable aspect of the experience of consciousness was projected not only inwards onto the soul, but outwards onto an independent objective reality. Most of the time this does not really matter. If the voice forbids you to eat the flesh of swine, that's only a problem if you like bacon with your morning coffee, in which case you can turn the dial to a religion that promotes a different diet. The dietary or ritual side of religion is the least of our problems, however. You don't have to be religious to understand the power of a food fad or the comfort an ancient ceremony can provide. If the voice had confined itself to dietary restrictions and harmless ritual practices we would not give it a second thought. It is the fact that the voice told Abraham to murder his son that gives us pause. Having been in the religion business all my life, I've picked up the survival-skill of theological interpretation of stories like this; but it took a novelist to open my eyes to the horror that lurked behind the theological abstractions. The standard theological interpretation of the story of Abraham's obedience to the voice that commanded him to sacrifice his son is to applaud it as a splendid example of faith. Because he was prepared to murder his son for the sake of the voice, we are supposed to admire the

absoluteness of Abraham's obedience. I was taught that
obedience to God must override every other loyalty.
By that standard, what a paragon of faith Abraham was!
Would that I had that kind of rock-like obedience! But
what about Isaac? Where does he figure in this? Did
the voice bother to consult him before using him as a
device for testing his father's faith? It all sounds like an
ugly variant of the X that turns those subjected to it
into things and inculcates the kind of blind obedience
that can turn us into evil robots. Is God to be thought
of as the Ultimate X, the Big Force, which is colossally
indifferent to everything except its own drives?

It was not theologians who made me ask these questions, but artists and people of the imagination. The
novelist I just mentioned was so appalled by the stories
religious folk told each other that she decided to expose
the horror of it in a fiction. Rather than seeing things
from God's angle, dealing in theological abstractions,
such as faith and obedience, in her novel *After these
Things* Jenny Diski imaginatively explores the human
side of these interactions. In particular, she gets inside
the head of Isaac, the unconsidered object of his father's
trial of faith. As Abraham hung over him, about to cut
his throat, Isaac must have realised that he lived in a
dangerous and unpredictable universe in which a son
might be sacrificed to the demands of a voice in his
father's head that was more powerful than any human
love. To put it another way, you can't trust a believer,
even if he is your father. That is the devastating insight
that makes the secular mind anxious about the unpredictable power religion has to plunge people into evil

madness. How can you negotiate the intricacies of living alongside people who are programmed by an invisible inaudible voice? And the voice is still at work, calling its servants to kill their children and ours in obedience to an allegiance that is more powerful than any human bond. We see it there three thousand years ago in the pages of the Bible; and we see it here today in the pages of our newspapers. The voice still speaks, and Abraham's children obey its command. The Terror of Isaac, the Bible's name for God, is still in business messing with people's heads.

But rather than issuing a block dismissal of all religion as dangerous fantasy, the psychotic residue of traumatic early experience, a more hopeful and positive approach suggests itself. In my own wrestling with religion I have found it helpful to think of it as a product of the human imagination, something that is self-enclosed and self-disclosed, not something that points away from itself to a transcendent reality. We do not have to take religion at its own valuation to get value out of it. If religion is a human invention, an examination of it will give us valuable information about ourselves and our strange story. This understanding of religion need not reduce its value to the user, any more than Auden's acknowledgement of the lowly source of his poetry diminishes its worth to the reader. It does mean, however, that we will value it in a different way and for different reasons. We will be less interested in the alleged divine authority of its origins, than in the gifts of interpretation it offers us for understanding our own lives. Lewis Hyde captures this mysterious commerce well in his book, *The Gift: How the Creative Spirit Transforms the World*. This is how he describes the transaction between us and the artist:

> A work of art that enters us to feed the soul offers to initiate in us the process of the gifted self which some antecedent gift initiated in the poet. Reading the work, *we* feel gifted for a while, and to the degree that we are able, we respond by creating new work (not art, perhaps, but with the artist's work at hand we suddenly find we can make sense of our own experience). The greatest art offers us images by which to imagine our lives. And once the imagination has been awakened, it is procreative: through it we can give more than we were given, say more than we had to say. This is one reason we cannot read an artist's work by his life. We learn something when we read the life, of course, but the true artist leaves us with the uncanny sense that the experience fails to explain the creation.[79]

The uncanny sense that the experience or humanity of artists fails to explain the astonishing creations that come through them applies to religion as well. We know enough about the origins of religion and its ugly history to be wary of it, maybe even revolted by it; but we also have to acknowledge that from that seething refuse tip some wonderful blossoms have bloomed – justice and mercy, love and forgiveness, as well as a whole gallery of tropes and metaphors that have helped us make sense of our own experience and manage our lives better. Even when it is most confident about its theoretical claim, religion is always aware of the fragility of the human mediators who act as its conduits to the world.

One of the most touching expressions of this is the idea of the wounded healer or damned redeemer. This is the theme of Graham Greene's greatest novel, *The Power and the Glory*. Greene liked to operate at the dangerous edge of theology, that mysterious boundary where the curse becomes a blessing and the man fleeing God brings God to others. 'He saved others; himself he cannot save,'[80] was what the mob chanted at Jesus on the cross, and it is not infrequently the dilemma of the artist and the priest. Mediators of grace to others, their own lives are often characterised by turbulence and tumult. The romantic in me wonders if this brokenness may not be the mysterious ingredient that is transmuted into grace through the priestly work of art. Certainly, some of the most creative priests and artists have been aware of belonging to a covenant of the wounded. That is why Tennessee Williams said he was afraid to exorcise his demons in case he lost his angels. In his prologue to *Cat on a Hot Tin Roof* he developed the idea.

Of course, it is a pity that so much of all creative work is so closely related to the personality of the one who does it. It is sad and embarrassing and unattractive that those emotions that stir him deeply enough to demand expression, and to charge that expression with some measure of light and power, are nearly all rooted, however changed in their surface, in the particular and sometimes peculiar concerns of the artist himself, that special world, the passions and images of it that each of us weaves about him from birth to death, a web of monstrous complexity, spun forth at a speed that is incalculable to a length beyond measure, from the spider mouth of his own singular perceptions . . . Personal lyricism is the outcry of prisoner to prisoner from the cell in solitary where each is confined for the duration of his life.[81]

I want to look at an example from one of Williams' plays, *The Night of the Iguana*, which, to me, exemplifies that outcry of prisoner to prisoner that often lies behind the creative act. It comes in Act III. Shannon, the disgraced Episcopal minister, is quizzing Hannah about her love life. She tells him there had only been two incidents, the first a brief encounter in a cinema when she was sixteen, when a young man had sat down beside her and pushed his knees against hers. The second had been only a couple of years ago. A middle-aged Australian ladies' underwear salesman had paid generously for one of her watercolours. Later that evening he had invited her out on a sampan and, because of his earlier generosity, she accepted. This is how the scene continues:

HANNAH: . . . I noticed that he became more and more . . .
SHANNON: What?
HANNAH: Well . . . *agitated* . . . as the afterglow of the sunset faded out on the water. [*She laughs with delicate sadness.*] Well, finally, eventually, he leaned towards me . . . we were *vis-à-vis* in the sampan . . . and he looked intensely, passionately into my eyes. [*She laughs again.*] And he said to me: 'Miss Jelkes? Will you do me a favour? Will you do something for me?' 'What?' said I. 'Well,' said he, 'if I turn my back, if I look the other way, will you take off some piece of your clothes and let me hold it, just hold it?' . . . Then he said, 'It will just take a few seconds.' 'Just a few seconds for what?'

I asked him. [*She gives the same laugh again.*] He didn't
say for what, but . . .
SHANNON: His satisfaction?
HANNAH: Yes.

Hannah accedes to the Australian's request. He keeps
his promise, turns his back, and she slips off an intimate
part of her underwear. Politely, she looks the other way
while his satisfaction takes place. She goes on:

HANNAH: . . . The incident was embarrassing, not
violent. I left and returned unmolested. Oh, and the
funniest part of all is that when we got back to
the Raffles Hotel, he took the piece of apparel out of
his pocket like a bashful boy producing an apple for his
school-teacher and tried to slip it into my hand in
the elevator. I wouldn't accept it. I whispered, 'Oh,
please keep it Mr Willoughby!' He'd paid the asking
price for one of my water-colors and somehow the
little experience had been rather touching. I mean it
was *lonely*, out there in the sampan with violet streaks
in the sky and this little middle-aged Australian making
sounds like he was dying of asthma! And the planet
Venus coming serenely out of a fair-weather cloud,
over the Straits of Malacca . . .
SHANNON: And that experience . . . you call that a . . .
HANNAH: A love experience? Yes. I do call it one . . .
[*He regards her with incredulity, peering into her face so closely
that she is embarrassed and becomes defensive.*]
SHANNON: That, that . . . sad, dirty little episode, you
call it a . . . ?
HANNAH: [*cutting in sharply*]: Sad it certainly was – for
the odd little man – but why do you call it 'dirty'?
SHANNON: You mean it didn't disgust you?
HANNAH: Nothing human disgusts me unless it's

unkind, violent. And I told you how gentle he was . . .
apologetic, shy, and really very, well, *delicate* about it.[82]

'Nothing human disgusts me unless it's unkind, violent.'
The bleakness of Tennessee Williams' plays are lit with
little acts of wistful understanding and forgiving kindness like that, encounters he describes in the same play
as 'broken gates between people so they can reach each
other, even if it's just for one night only'.[83] A few
moments before she'd described her encounter with the
Australian fetishist, Hannah had been trying to reach
out over their broken gates to the troubled Shannon.
She told him she respected a person like him, 'who had
to fight and howl . . . for his decency and his bit of
goodness, much more than I respect the lucky ones that
just had theirs handed out to them at birth and never
afterwards snatched from them by . . . unbearable . . .
torments'.[84] The 'unbearable torment' in the lives of
great artists is sometimes transmuted into a sweeping
compassion for the human condition. Though this does
not account for what Hyde called the artists' 'antecedent
gift' for making great art, it certainly informs and infuses
it. That is why it is legitimate to see Williams' compassion for the haunted losers in his plays as the fruit of
his own torments. If you had exorcised his demons, you
would have destroyed his angels.

A related point was made by Margaret Drabble, who
said that Philip Larkin cheers us up because he recon-
ciles us to our ills by the scrupulous way in which he
notices them.[85] The same can be said of religion, and
one way to use it is to observe how it notices and

responds creatively to the tensions in the human condition. Hugh Walpole said that the world was a comedy
for those who think, a tragedy for those who feel: any
scrupulous noticing of the ills of the world must hold
both ends of that polarity. One of the consolations of
literature is the way it transmutes the tragic comedy of
life into art by *noticing* it. The same can be said of exist
ential religion. The genius of a sane religious sensibility
is the way its myth-making keeps the balance between
tragedy and comedy, pessimism and optimism, the former
saving us from the intoxicating dangers of utopian
thinking, the latter saving us from the despairing immo-
bilism that denies any possibility of hope.

The first note in the redemption song of Christianity
is dark, and proclaims a profound pessimism about the
human condition. Christianity has been rightly denounced
for some of the ways it has applied its doctrine of the
Fall, which is why it is better to see it not as a doctrine
but as an eloquent metaphor for the ills to which we are
constitutionally prone: a way of noticing.

> The troubles of our proud and angry dust
> Are from eternity, and shall not fail.[86]

The myth of the Fall flows from a way of reading the
great Hebrew myth of Eden. It is silly to historicise the
myth, as literalists do. It misses the point to see it as some
kind of historical claim about human origins. A myth is
a narrative that carries existential truth. Myth is art, the
bearer of meaning through mystery. It reflects us back to
ourselves, which is why we should never lose touch with

it if we want to understand the enigma of our own existence. The myth of the Fall reflects an enduring theme in
human experience, which is why it is constantly revisited
in great fiction. Even if we have never read the original
myth of the Fall in its biblical setting, we will have encountered its truth when it surfaces in other forms. One of its
most poignant recent expressions comes at the end of Alan
Hollinghurst's great novel, *The Line of Beauty*. Nick, who
is waiting for the result of an HIV test, has just been
banished from the Feddens' large house in Notting Hill,
after an enormous scandal has engulfed the family, and for
which he has been unfairly blamed. He muses as he walks
away from the front door.

It came over him that the result would be positive. The
words that were said every day to others would be said
to him, in that quiet consulting room whose desk and
carpet and square modern armchair would share indis-
solubly in the moment . . . What would he do once he
left the room? He dawdled on rather breathless, seeing
visions in the middle of the day. He tried to ration-
alize the fear, but its pull was too strong and original.
It was inside himself, but the world around him, the
parked cars, the cruising taxi, the church spire among
the trees, had also been changed. They had been revealed.
It was like a drug sensation, but without the awareness
of play . . . The emotion was startling. It was a sort of
terror, made up of emotions from every stage of his
short life, weaning, homesickness, envy and self-pity;
but he felt that the self-pity belonged to a larger pity.
It was a love of the world that was shockingly unconditional. He stared back at the house, and then
turned and drifted on. He looked in bewilderment at

number 24, the final house with its regalia of stucco
swags and bows. It wasn't just this street corner but the
fact of a street corner at all that seemed, in the light
of the moment, so beautiful.[87]

A larger pity . . . Moments of extremity like that can
reveal the world to us – 'the fact of a street corner at
all' – and our shockingly unconditional love of it. And
we can build a partial understanding of the human condition on this tragic vision. The ills of existence crowd in
on us unbidden, but we increase their power over us by
harbouring delusions about ourselves and others. Humans
certainly ought to posit ideals for themselves, but the sad
fact is that we constantly fail them or are failed by them.
It has something to do with the endemic discontents we
suffer from, but it has more to do with our ignorance
of the inner dynamics of our own nature.

The classic expression of the Fall in the New Testament
is the story of Simon Peter, Jesus' right-hand man. There
is no doubt that Peter loved and admired Jesus, and the
gospels are noisy with his protestations of loyalty and
determination to follow him to death. There is no need
to doubt the sincerity of his avowals, any more than we
should doubt the sincerity of the average couple who
pledge to live with each other till death, but end up separ-
ating. In time we learn that we neither fully understand
the hidden imperatives of our own souls, nor are we in
command of the circumstances that lie ahead of us in
the future. This may have been why Jesus warned against
taking oaths and making promises. To do so is to command
the wind and the seas. Jesus understood that sincerity

was no guarantee of fidelity. One of the most poignant phrases in world literature is found in Luke's gospel just after Peter's third denial of the man he had promised to die for. Luke tells us: 'And the Lord turned, and looked upon Peter. And Peter remembered the word of the Lord, how he had said unto him, Before the cock crow, thou shalt deny me thrice. And Peter went out, and wept bitterly.'[88] Peter's tragedy was not lack of sincerity; it was an incapacity to fulfil the pledge he had sincerely made. We create these heartbreaks for ourselves time after time in life, but we make them worse by our failure to recognise that they are the rule not the exception. All our paradises are lost paradises. The way we let unrealistic expectations destroy flawed yet retrievable relationships is sad enough; a bigger hazard of our Edenic fantasies is when we transpose them onto the collective level, whether in religion or politics. More misery and disillusionment has been visited on humanity by its search for the perfect society and the perfect faith than by any other cause. The fantasy of crafting the ideal society or establishing the perfect religious system is far from being an endearing form of romanticism: it all too easily turns into terror. Listening to the voice that commands us to follow its perfect blueprint for rebuilding Eden usually results not in heaven but in hell on earth, whether in the home-grown or a built-for-export version.

Applying the wisdom of the Fall to interpersonal relationships commits us to a life of forgiving, including self-forgiving. Applying it in the wider sphere of national and international relations commits us to political modesty. It is not sufficiently acknowledged that the idea of the

Fall lies behind some of our best political experiments, such as liberal democracy. The kind of society we have evolved in northern Europe, flawed though it is, has three redeeming characteristics, the first of which is a healthy mistrust of power and those who wield it. It knows, of course, that power has to be exercised if society is to function, but it is well aware, from its understanding of human history, that power is an invariably corrupting experience for humans. The adaptive response to this insight was twofold. First was the principle of reversibility: never give people power over you until you know how to get rid of them. Related to this was the gradual erection of checks and balances within and between the power centres themselves. Associated with this realism about the corrupting effects of power was the emergence of tolerance as a fundamental ethical imperative in plural societies: not a grudging decision to rub along with people you disagree with, but something that was almost celebratory in its acknowledgement that human variety and difference are positively good for the human community. Another characteristic of the liberal democratic style is the conviction that it is wrong to harm people. We will all disagree heatedly over the best way to do good to people and whether we are under any obligation even to attempt it; but most of us will agree about the importance of not harming them and are likely to agree, too, on the simple ethical basis of such a principle: never do to others what you would not like them to do to you.

If the idea of the Fall and the Expulsion from Eden is the *yin* of the great biblical myths, then the idea of the Return is the *yang*. It is found in the great Hebrew myth of the Exodus from Egypt, which gets expressed in Christian scriptures in the idea of resurrection. Its most tender expression in the New Testament is the story of the restoration of Peter, found in the Gospel of John. After the crucifixion of Jesus and his own desertion of him, Peter goes back to his old job as a fisherman on the Sea of Galilee. It takes a poet like George Mackay Brown to capture the hope and regret of the scene:

> Fishermen with hands burned
> From rasp of rope and rowlock
> Out on the lake,
> Who is the man in the last light,
> At the fire-glimmer, on shore stones
> Poaching fish in a pot?
>
> It is the man they hooked
> On the dead tree.[89]

With the supreme tact of the artist, John shows, but doesn't tell what happened next in the encounter between Peter and the man on the shore:

Jesus saith to Simon Peter, Simon, son of Jonas, lovest thou me more than these? He saith unto him, Yea, Lord; thou knowest that I love thee. He saith unto him, Feed my lambs. He saith unto him again the second time, Simon, son of Jonas, lovest thou me? He saith unto him, Yea, Lord; thou knowest that I love thee. He saith unto him, Feed my sheep. He saith unto him the third time, Simon, son of Jonas, lovest thou me? Peter was grieved because he said unto him the third time, Lovest thou me? And he said unto him, Lord, thou

knowest all things; thou knowest that I love thee. Jesus
saith unto him, Feed my sheep.[90]

There is no mention of the betrayals, but there is an
opportunity to repeat the avowals, the sincere avowals
that shattered on the rock of Peter's weakness. Peter was
not a monster, a vicious man: vice is unconscious of itself.
Peter was a weak man: and weakness is all too conscious
of itself. What Jesus restored to Peter was the gift to go
on failing without being destroyed by it. This is what
forgiveness does, and it was the central message of Jesus.
Peter's threefold renewal of his broken vows could not
repair his three denials: one cannot undo the past. But
it gave him the possibility of a different future. Apart
from the damage our failures do to others, their main
offence is the way they trap us in constant remembrance
of times past. By persuading us to give up all hope of a
better past, forgiveness gives us the possibility of a better
future, and replaces despair with hope. Again, we miss
the existential point of the encounter between Peter and
the risen Jesus if we start fretting about its historicity.
Who can tell what kind of event we are dealing with?
It could have been an event in the mind of Peter who
suddenly, after Jesus died, got the message he so con-
spicuously failed to grasp while he lived: that without
forgiveness the tragedy of the human condition is com-
pounded, and that he had better begin by forgiving himself.
The important thing about hope is not *how* it comes
back, but that it does come back, again and again. The
cruellest act in the vast repertoire of human cruelty is the
denial of hope; and the kindest act is its restoration.

If the restoration of personal and social hope through constant forgiveness is one element in the myth of the Return, then the other is just as important: while monsters may triumph in real time, in the long reach of history they are usually defeated. They may kill the poet; they can never kill the poem. They may – and usually do – kill the prophet; they can never kill the memory of his challenge to the powerful. One way to get my meaning is by intentionally misinterpreting the Latin translation of Hippocrates' famous aphorism: *ars longa, vita brevis*. Art, including spiritual wisdom, endures long after tyrants have gone under the hill. Art alone cannot save us from ourselves, of course, but it can be a part of what does. According to the great German pessimist Arthur Schopenhauer, the world is a cruel place that devours its children and cares little for their pains. Only two things, he believed, can help us to minimise the horror: one is the capacity for pity, the other is art. I would go slightly further than Schopenhauer and claim that art, in which I include the existential understanding of religion, can increase our pity by helping us to enter imaginatively into the lives of others. It is no accident that the great monsters of history have all hated pity. In a speech to the National Convention in Paris on 26th February, 1794, at the height of the Terror, Robespierre went so far as to say, 'Pity is treason.' The arts not only prompt us to the kind of treasonous pity that opposes the men enraged or intoxicated by power, they are also likely to be our most enduring memorial. When we are gone and forgotten, and the captains and the kings have all departed, the work of the best artists will remain as witness to our generation's fleeting moment on earth. More importantly, in time enduring art overshadows the great monsters who bestrode the world. This was the point Shelley made in 'Ozymandias of Egypt':

> I met a traveller from an antique land
> Who said: Two vast and trunkless legs of stone
> Stand in the desert. Near them on the sand,
> Half sunk, a shattered visage lies, whose frown
> And wrinkled lip and sneer of cold command,
> Tell that its sculptor well those passions read
> Which yet survive, stamped on these lifeless things,
> The hand that mocked them, and the heart that fed.
> And on the pedestal these words appear:
> 'My name is Ozymandias, king of kings:
> Look on my works, ye Mighty, and despair!'
> Nothing beside remains: round the decay
> Of that colossal wreck, boundless and bare,
> The lone and level sands stretch far away.[91]

Nothing would be remembered of Ozymandias, king of kings, were it not for the sculptor who captured his sneer of cold command and the poet who told his story. And who would remember Pontius Pilate today had he not signed the death warrant for a travelling preacher of moral genius in the province of Judea towards the end of his time as Governor? The myth of the Return does not save us from tragedy – the crucifixions go on – but it reminds us never to respect those who may kill our bodies but can never kill our souls.

The creative tension between the two great myths of Expulsion and Return is found not only in the religion that imagined them, but in universal human experience. Inevitably, since holding any kind of tension is difficult for us, we usually resolve the difficulty by moving to one end or the other – or maybe we are moved by factors, including our temperaments, that are beyond our control. Individuals, as well as religions and whole societies, can be crudely divided into those that emphasise the Fall and those that emphasise the possibilities of restoration; between those that say a forbidding 'No' to human hope, and those that say a forgiving 'Yes'. And art itself lives within the pull of this tension, especially literature. In *The Unquiet Grave* Cyril Connolly wrote something that has haunted me since I first came across it: 'There are but two ways to be a great writer: like Homer, Shakespeare or Goethe to accept life completely, or like Pascal, Proust, Leopardi, Baudelaire, to refuse ever to lose sight of its horror.'[92]

The Yes and the No. Both religion and art stand astonished before the being of being, the there-ness, this-ness, that-ness of things – the fact that there is a street corner at all – and they respond with both wonder and horror. The artist's way of noticing heightens and concentrates the there-ness of things. Yes, and the strangeness of things. 'Rilke said of Cézanne that he did not paint, "I like it," he painted, "There it is." '[93] There is a fine example of this in Proust's account of the death of Bergotte, a fiction-alised version of himself. Bergotte loved Vermeer's *View of Delft*, a picture he thinks he has completely mem-orised. But a critic has just praised the perfection of 'a little patch of yellow wall' that Bergotte cannot

remember, so he goes to see it again. This is how
Proust describes the scene:

> He remembered [it] as more brilliant, more distinctive
> than anything else he knew, but in which, thanks to the
> critic's article, he remarked for the first time little human
> figures in blue, the pinkness of the sand, and finally the
> precious tiny patch of yellow on the wall. His giddi-
> ness increased; he fixed his eyes, like a child on a yellow
> butterfly which it wants to catch, upon the precious
> little patch of wall. 'That is how I ought to have written,'
> he said. 'My last books are too dry. I should have kept
> overlaying them with more colour, made my sentences
> more finely-wrought, like this little patch of yellow wall.'
> Meanwhile he realised the gravity of his physical faint-
> ness. It appeared to him that on the heavenly scales were
> balanced, on one side, his own life, on the other the
> little patch of wall so beautifully painted in yellow. He
> repeated to himself: 'Little patch of yellow on the wall;
> little patch of yellow on the wall.' While doing so he
> sank down upon a circular settee . . . A new stroke beat
> him down, he rolled off the settee to the floor, as visit-
> ors and attendants rushed towards him.[94]

In contrast to the art that passionately *notices* things, such
as a little patch of yellow on a wall, religion has a fatal
weakness for trying to *explain* them. But if you abandon
religion's explanatory function, you can sometimes get
religion itself back as an art that, though it refuses ever
to lose sight of life's horror, is also equipped by the deep
wisdom of its myths to accept it completely. Behind the
architecture of religious myth in its pessimistic mode can
be heard a great 'No' to the crimes and follies of humanity.

Taken as a metaphor, an imaginative construct, the myth of the Fall fits the reality of the human condition: 'the horror, the horror'.[95] There is a fiction of original sin, a refusal ever to lose sight of that horror, and some of humanity's best writing belongs to it. But in the midst of the horror, people can still reach out to each other over broken gates. We need both forms of religious and artistic honesty today, the Yes and the No; but I believe we are in greater need of the Yes. I have no reason to suppose that individuals are less forgiving than they ever were, less disposed to reach out to others over broken gates, but there is something ugly and unforgiving about our common culture at the moment, reflected in the gleeful vindictiveness of sections of the press at the tragic weaknesses of public figures. That is why I am proud that it was the melancholy Scottish poet Iain Crichton Smith who told us it was 'from our own weakness only are we kind' and went on to remind us that it is never too late 'to forgive our poor journey and our common grave'.[96]

Earlier I described Hugh Walpole's aphorism that life was a comedy for those who think and a tragedy for those who feel as another version of history's *yin* and *yang*, the Fall and the Return: but maybe what we need today is less emphasis on the tragic sense of life and more on the comic sense of life. In 1974, while the war in Vietnam was grinding on, an English professor called Joseph Meeker wrote a book called *The Comedy of Survival*. Intriguingly, it combined literary criticism with a look at animal behaviour. He offered a way of looking at the world and a strategy for living he called 'the comic way'. He had noticed that while comedy was not necessarily

humorous it did contrast sharply with the tragic view of
life, which tended to manufacture abstract moralities and
engage in the kind of power struggles that inevitably
ended in disaster. In contrast to the human animal, he
claimed that the workings of the natural world are essentially comic. They are about durability, survival and, most
importantly, reconciliation. Evolution, Meeker wrote,

> ... proceeds as an unscrupulous, opportunistic comedy,
> the object of which appears to be the proliferation and
> preservation of as many life forms as possible. Successful
> participants in it are those who live and reproduce even
> when times are hard and dangerous, not those who are
> best able to destroy enemies or competitors. Its ground
> rules for participants, including people, are those that also
> govern literary comedy; organisms must adapt themselves
> to their circumstances in every possible way, must studiously
> avoid all-or-nothing choices, must seek alternatives to
> death, must accept and revel in maximum diversity, must
> accommodate themselves to the accidental limitations of
> birth and environment, yet compete successfully when
> necessary ... Comedy is a strategy for living that contains
> ecological wisdom, and it may be one of our best guides
> as we try to retain a place for ourselves among other
> animals that live according to the comic way.[97]

In his discussion of this passage, Richard Mabey[98]
reminds us that the ultimate expression of the comic
way is play (including what humans call art), an almost
universal phenomenon among more complex animals,
and one which, in its exuberant purposelessness, comes
as close as we can get to understanding the meaning
of life. Play, art, exuberant purposelessness: these can

certainly strengthen our love of life and of the others
with whom we share it; and they can even help us
befriend the sorrow that always accompanies us on our
journey towards the grave. The beauty of this insight is
that it encourages us to notice and learn from the other
animals with whom we share the planet, whose lives
and significance we so cruelly disdain. We have tyran-
nised them and have come close to destroying ourselves
by the lust for purpose our big brains have lured us
into. Our addiction to purpose, our passion for meaning,
trap us in contempt for those who follow different
purposes, pursue other meanings. But what if there is
no ultimate religious or perfect political meaning to
life? What if the meaning of life is life itself, and the
living of it wisely and tenderly is the only purpose we
can give it? Then the comic way might save us from
ourselves by persuading us to take ourselves less seri-
ously. Just as importantly, it might just save the earth
and the other creatures we share it with. We don't know
why the earth, our sustaining yet indifferent mother,
bore us; and she probably doesn't know either: but here
we are, thrown into the exuberant purposelessness of
being. It seems a pity not to enjoy it for its own sake.
But before we can contemplate that happy state we are
going to have to think again about the monsters who
stamp on human joy – and about the remarkable people,
few in any generation, who resist them.

6

SAINT

He who does not recognise to what extent shifting fortune and necessity hold in subjection every human spirit, cannot regard as fellow-creatures nor love as he loves himself those whom chance separated from him by an abyss. Only he who has measured the dominion of force, and knows how not to respect it, is capable of love and justice.

SIMONE WEIL

When I was an insufferable young seminarian, part of my daily devotional discipline was to read from cloying volumes of hagiography. There were a number of biographical dictionaries available which provided a short reading about the saints on their day in the liturgical calendar. The format was pretty standard. There would be a chronological outline of the saint's life, an account of the miracles he or she had performed – the ability to work miracles being a constitutive part of sainthood – the date of death, and a list of objects for which the saint's prayers were reckoned to be efficacious. Years later, in a rueful sermon I preached about lessons I had learnt from this phase of youthful piety, I confected a fictional example of the kind of thing I used to come across.

Saint Prigissimus, born in Whitby in 607 to devout parents, was noted for his piety from an early age. At the age of five he insisted on sewing thorns into his shirt in order to identify with our Lord's sufferings. His first miracle was performed when he was seven, upon his uncle, a coarse and licentious man, much afflicted with stones in the kidney: upon receiving a godly admonition from his saintly nephew to amend his sinful life, the uncle spontaneously emitted the stones at the young boy's feet, to the praise and wonder of the onlookers. When he was nine years old, Prigissimus refused henceforth to look at members of the opposite sex, including his own mother and sisters. Thereafter, whenever he encountered a female he pulled his hood over his face and looked steadfastly upon the earth in order to preserve his purity from their lascivious gaze. At eleven, he miraculously struck two of his schoolfellows dumb for blasphemously mocking him. He entered the Monastery of the Great Yawn on his thirteenth birthday, and was made Abbot when he was seventeen. He lived on turnips and cold water till he was twenty-eight, when he died in great agony, though without complaint. He was canonised in 697 and is the patron saint of those who suffer from irritable bowel syndrome, for the relief of which his prayers are particularly efficacious. His emblem is the turnip and his day of commemoration is February 30th.

Behind the formulaic convention of that fictional description lies a whole theory of life that is as far from the unconditional love of the world we found at the end of Hollinghurst's novel – 'the fact of a street corner at all' – as it is possible to get. Extreme asceticism of the sort outlined in the excerpt is based on unconditional hatred of the world, lest its blandishments lure the soul away from its lonely ascent to God. This is an extreme version of the old anxiety I have already referred to: how can we enjoy the pleasures of the senses without being totally overpowered by them? While it is certainly true that some of us are bad at controlling what the Christian ascetical tradition disparagingly describes as our 'carnal appetites', what is often overlooked is that personal experience of the weakness of the flesh can inoculate us against harsher compulsions to judge and dominate others. Iain Crichton Smith has already reminded us that 'from our own weakness only are we kind'. One of the sweetest ironies of the spiritual life is that honest acceptance of our own lack of self-control may be the only thing that keeps us from trying to control others. In this book I am not using 'saint' in anything like its traditional sense, especially if it is associated with the denials that characterise asceticism. Indeed, it could be argued that the constant struggle to deny ourselves the pleasures of life usually only results in the development of a strained and overwrought personality. After all, Hitler was an ascetic, but he was also one of the greatest monsters of the twentieth century. Maybe if he had really known how to enjoy himself the history of the twentieth century would have been very different. Anyway, I shall give the word saint different shades of meaning in this chapter, but none of them will look anything like poor Prigissimus.

The word 'saint' in New Testament Greek is *hagios*. Originally, it referred to objects, such as pots and bowls, that were set apart for a sacred or holy use in worship. In time it was applied to the whole people of Israel, because it was believed they had been set apart by God for a particular purpose. At this stage the word still lacks any resonance of heightened or perfected character or conduct. It is a functional word that denotes a particular role, the way one might set apart an old pair of trousers for gardening duty rather than throwing them away. Christianity borrowed the word from Judaism – as it borrowed much else – and in time it got moralised and associated, though not exclusively, with heroic self-denial. Nevertheless, the core meaning at the heart of the word is still useful: there are people who are different from the rest of us; they are set apart, either by circumstance or character, to confront and speak truth to human monsters who trample on the joy of others. To be precise: they challenge those humans who have allowed themselves to be completely taken over by force and have become heartless instruments of the domination of others. Most of us are likely to be cowed or hypnotised by the glamour of power in its many manifestations. The set-apart person, the *saint* in this specialised sense, is unimpressed by any of it. In Simone Weil's words, they have measured the dominion of force and know how not to respect it. Such people are rare in any generation, and they usually suffer for their courage. One of the bravest of them was Osip Mandelstam, a Russian Jew who was arrested in 1934 for writing a poem about Joseph Stalin.

We live, deaf to the land beneath us,
Ten steps away no one hears our speeches.

All we hear is the Kremlin mountaineer,
The murderer and peasant-slayer.

His fingers are fat as grubs
And the words, final as lead weights, fall from his lips,

His cockroach whiskers leer
And his boot tops gleam.

Around him a rabble of thin-necked leaders –
fawning half-men for him to play with.

They whinny, purr or whine
As he prates and points a finger,

One by one forging his laws, to be flung
Like horseshoes at the head, to the eye or the groin.

And every killing is a treat
For the broad-chested Ossette.[99]

Ossette was a reference to a rumour that Stalin came from
Iranian stock in northern Georgia. In the poem that cost
him his life, Mandelstam put his finger on the most insidious effect power has on weak men: 'fawning half-men
for him to play with'. Apart from those who are reduced
to thing-hood in its most literal form in death by the
men of power, most people are bent out of shape by its
various manifestations, including relatively benign ones.
Study photographs of people meeting the royals; observe
junior members of Parliament in the presence of the
Prime Minister; watch visiting bishops in the presence of
the Pope: their skeletons melt, they become smilingly soft
and compliant, goofy-looking; they lose moral definition.
The force of the visiting presence turns them into things.
It is very difficult to resist this effect. Even if you are one
of those puritans who are self-righteously resistant to being
over-awed, the fact that you are having to put energy into
being unimpressed shows that you too have been bent

out of shape by force. And those who have been totally taken over by it and purged of all human sympathy hate any challenge to their preening authority. Mandelstam was arrested for his poem about the Kremlin mountaineer, the murderer and peasant-slayer. He died in a labour camp in 1938.

The central question of this book, which I believe to be the central question facing humanity, is to what extent we will let force in any of its forms turn us into people who treat others as things, however limited the compass of our influence. In chapter one we noticed how sex, in particular, lends itself to this kind of objectification; but one of the many paradoxes of sexual need is that a rueful acknowledgement of its power over us can prompt us to lives of greater kindness. Honestly owning the extent to which we ourselves have been victims of force can help us refuse ever to victimise others. Andrea Dworkin explored the liberating possibility of this paradox in *Intercourse*. In chapter three, 'Stigma', she gives us a moving analysis of another of Tennessee Williams' plays, *A Streetcar Named Desire*. In her reading of this text, Dworkin discovers a possible way of transcending the relentless pressure of the life force upon our fragile humanity. It is found in the contrast between Stanley – the perfect expression of remorseless, brute sexuality – and the vulnerable Blanche, whose promiscuity is actually a search for a haven of gentleness in a rough world. This is how Williams describes Stanley:

> Animal joy in his being is implicit in all his movements and attitudes. Since earliest manhood the centre of his

life has been pleasure with women, the giving and
taking of it, not with weak indulgence, dependently,
but with the power and pride of a richly feathered
male bird among hens.[100]

Stanley has no interior life, is incapable of feeling, of iden-
tifying with the pain and suffering of others, unlike his
sister-in-law Blanche, who is marked by a strong capacity
for feeling. Compared to Stanley's animal sexuality, Blanche
has a distinctly human aptitude for suffering the internal
consequences of sex and love, especially the loneliness and
remorse that often accompany them. Dworkin describes
her as having 'an indelible human sorrow, perhaps a distinctly
human incapacity to heal, because some kinds of pain do
not lessen in the human heart'.[101] Blanche has reached the
end of the line: her teaching job is gone because she was
found morally unfit, after having sex with a seventeen-
year-old student; her land is gone, eaten up by debt; and
her sexual adventuring, what she calls 'intimacies with
strangers', is over, because she is worn-out. Longing to
find a cleft in the rock of the world in which to hide, she
is hoping Mitch – Stanley's card-playing buddy – will
marry her, but that depends on maintaining the lie of her
gentility, of being a lady, of never having ridden on that
streetcar named Desire. When Mitch learns the truth about
her, he discards her; and tells her she's not clean enough
to be in the same house as his mother. At the conclusion
of the play, while his wife Stella is in hospital having their
baby, Stanley rapes Blanche. Dworkin writes:

Because Stanley has no interior life of feeling, he has no
remorse; the rape is just another fuck for him . . . Blanche

pays the price for having a human sexuality and a human
consciousness . . . For her, sex was part of a human quest
for human solace, human kindness . . . Stanley, ordinary,
unrepressed, was the natural enemy of sex with any dimension of human longing or human meaning, any wanting
that was not just for the raw, cold, hard fuck, a sensual
using without any edge of loneliness or discontent.[102]

Stella rejects her sister's version of what took place. This
rejection snaps Blanche's unsteady hold on reality, making
it easy for Stanley to have her locked away in an insane
asylum, a tactic that has been a frequent response of male
authority to the emotionally awkward concomitants of
female sexuality. From the placing of 'fallen' women in
Magdalene laundries to their incarceration in mental hospi-
tals, male authority has been brutally effective at hushing
up and covering over the embarrassing consequences of
its own lusts.

Dworkin believes that rescue from this cycle of brutal
meaninglessness comes through what she calls 'stigma',
from the Latin for 'mark', the Greek for 'tattoo', the plural
of which commonly refers to the marks or wounds on
the crucified Christ.[103] It is through suffering that we find
the possibility of resisting the implacable force that so
often threatens to smother us like sand.

The consequences to a human life of sex desired and
had are often pathetic, reducing the person to pathos.
Being marked by sexuality means that experience has
effects – that one is marked when one has been touched,
and the mark stays; that one is not new . . . Being marked
means that the sex has costs, and that one has paid . . .
The stigma is being set apart not by a vocation for sex

alone, but also perhaps by a vocation for human consequences – loss, suffering, despair, madness.[104]

Along with the pain sex can cause comes the possibility
of empathising with others, of seeing them as beings like
ourselves whose deepest fear is of being turned into things.
This sensitivity to others is close to Kant's 'categorical
imperative': 'For all rational beings stand under the law
that each of them should treat himself and all others never
merely as means but in every case also as an end in
himself.'[105] The saving paradox in all this is that the possible
remedy for the objectifying force of sexuality lies in
acknowledging that we ourselves have been marked and
made to suffer by it.

The suffering provoked by sexual need can be the clue
to its humanising and gentling, but I wonder if it may
not also, on occasion, be the source of something more
profound: may it not be that the experience of what
Dworkin calls the sexual wound can dispose some who
are marked by it to challenge those who wield a more
deadly power? I am thinking of two remarkable Christian
ministers – saints in my sense of the term, because they
dedicated themselves to the overthrow of tyranny – who
were wounded by their own sexual needs, yet challenged
the powerful at great cost to themselves. Martin Luther
King was the Moses figure of the civil rights movement
in the USA: he brought his people close to the promised land, though he himself was never destined to enter
it himself. King hoped that one day America would live
up to the true meaning of its own creed 'that all men are
created equal'. In his most famous speech he dreamt that

one day in the red hills of Georgia the sons of former slaves would sit down at the table of brotherhood with the sons of former slave owners. The monster he challenged was a complex one. It was personalised in the form of racist sheriffs, governors and school principals, but its real power lay in its profound and almost immovable rooting in the institutional life of the nation he set out to change. The story of his challenge to that many-headed monster and the price he paid for making it are too well-known to need repeating here. What we have only discovered slowly over the years since his death was that he also struggled with sexual needs that were inconsistent with the conventions of the church to which he belonged. His extra-marital sexual activities were secretly taped by the FBI and used against him.[106] He was assassinated before the information could be used publicly to smear him, though knowing he was being spied on added to the burden of his struggles not only with his own nature, but with the tentacles of the system he was challenging. A version of that history has recently repeated itself in Zimbabwe, where Catholic Archbishop Pius Ncube, one of the main voices of protest against the vanity and tyranny of Robert Mugabe, one of the monsters of post-colonial Africa, has recently been the victim of a government exposé of his sex life. The tragedy is that the video recording of the archbishop in bed with a woman, almost certainly obtained through the activities of the Central Investigation Organisation in Bulawayo, has succeeded in silencing one of Mugabe's most persistent and effective critics. The irony is that it was not a refutation of Ncube's challenge to the gross misgovernment of the Mugabe regime that was offered in reply to his accusations, but revelations about his love life. Given his official status as a celibate priest, it was probably impossible to expect Ncube to ride out the scandal by pointing to the absurdity of thinking that revelations about his own weakness could in any way invalidate his accusations against Mugabe, another Stalinesque peasant slayer. What the incident shows is how ruthless force is at defending itself, and how adept it is at playing the sex card when it suits it.

But politicians are far from being the only group playing the game of 'sex trumps every other moral issue on the planet'. Andrea Dworkin believes that the revival of religious fundamentalism in the world today is a fight-back by the male power group against the social and civil advances women have made in society. Though their language constantly refers to the divinely established order of things, Dworkin sees the traditionalist revolt as a straightforward attempt to restore male power. She says this inevitably involves a rigorous tightening of restraints on male sexual behaviour as well as intensifying civil and sexual controls on women.[107] Significantly, she believes that the opposition by traditionalists to recent civil and social liberties for homosexuals is the flipside of the same phenomenon. The Anglican Church is not the only religion struggling with this issue, though it is the only one doing so in the public square. Many commentators are baffled by the phenomenon of a traditionally inclusive communion tearing itself apart over the ecclesiastical status of men and women of homosexual orientation. Ironically, the land-grab against the ground gained by the emancipation of homosexuals in the Anglican Church is being led by bishops from Africa, where poverty and political corruption are far greater moral challenges than the sex life of bishops, however colourful or unorthodox. The bishops are playing the Mugabe card with a vengeance: ignore corruption, disease and criminal misgovernment, the only really important issue is what bishops get up to in their bedrooms. I got another wrinkle on this topic from a woman professor at a South African university I met at the Lambeth Conference in 1998: she told me that the best way to understand the revolt of African bishops against the liberalising of attitudes to homosexuality was as an assertion of male control of sexuality. One aspect of this has always been the traditional dominance of men over women, but the other has been the ancient prohibition of sodomy *because of the way it undermines the idea of male dominance.* Dworkin gets straight to the point as usual:

> Can sodomy become a legal form of intercourse without irredeemably compromising male power over women, that power being premised on men being entirely distinct from women in use, in function, in posture and position, in role, in 'nature'? Or will the legalisation of sodomy mortally injure the class power of men by sanctioning a fuck in which men are treated like women; the boundaries of men's bodies no longer being, as a matter of social policy and divine right, inviolate?[108]

The passionate intensity of the opposition to gay liberation by African bishops is psychologically significant. Christianity has usually managed to adapt itself to social developments, such as democracy, which was seen at first as inimical to its self-understanding; or the abolition of slavery, which was held to run counter to the clear testimony of scripture. The tell-tale sign that a psychological rather than a theological threat lurks beneath the surface of debate is the presence of anger. Virginia Woolf mused on why powerful men were *so angry* a lot of the time. It seemed absurd to her that the powerful should be angry, till it occurred to her that anger was always 'the familiar, the attendant sprite on power'.[109] Power gets angry when it is under threat. There are many activities, many practices, that divide opinion among humans, but the presence of anger usually tells us more about the state of the unconscious mind of the opponent than the practice opposed. We know, of course, that many homophobes turn out to be self-hating homosexuals – a phenomenon that is far from unknown in ecclesiastical circles. But the present angry torrent of hatred poured over gay men by African prelates is likely to have its origin in their contempt for sexual passivity in men, for their feminisation. The deeper contempt behind this hatred for gay men is probably for women themselves, because they are incapable of the fuck in this primordial sense. Men fuck. Women *get* fucked. QED.

Given the ruthless ferocity with which the powerful protect their right to dominate and control the private lives of others, what might save us from despair is to notice the existence of a number of countervailing pressures. In us the universe, this apparently purposeless explosion of blind power, has achieved consciousness and the ability to be an object to itself. An aspect of that consciousness is the ability not only to empathise with the victims of indifferent force, but the courage to challenge those who make themselves its instruments. No longer acting blindly, programmed by unconscious forces over which it has no control, in us the universe has achieved volition, however limited, and offers us the opportunity to alter the pre-determined course of events. In its way this is as big a mystery as the origin of the universe itself. We know that once there was nothing; then there was something: and we call that immeasurable quantitative shift a singularity. We also know that once there was blind indifference; then there was pity: and we call that immeasurable qualitative shift a singularity. Though we can account for neither event, in us they are actualised. If we are to survive and flourish we must work as hard at developing our capacity for empathy as we have at developing our capacity for rationality, so that we can resist and divert the imperious energies that threaten not only our own happiness and well-being, but our destruction as a species. We need not always suffer ourselves to be manipulated by force nor collude with our own domination; there is another approach we can take. It is very close to a process of personal transformation translated as repentance in the New Testament. The Greek word is *metanoia* from the verb *metanoien*, meaning to change one's mind. Obviously, it can be used of the simple process of reversing a previous decision, as in: 'I've changed my mind about driving to Inverness, and have decided to take the train instead.' Jesus used the word to describe a deeper kind of change, a transformation of character that is sometimes called con-version or reversing the direction of one's life. This is why translating *metanoia* as 'repentance', while limiting, is understandable. *Metanoia* invites us to engage in an act of radical self-examination that leads to the unflinching admission of what we have built from the life we were given and the choices we made. It is important to acknowledge both of the streams that contributed to the formation of our character: the factors beyond our control that predisposed us towards the choices we made; and the fact that *we* made the choices and were therefore complicit in our own bondage. This dialectical approach affirms both ends of the human paradox: we are certainly determined by factors that were never in our control, including the genetic lottery and our social and family environment; but the fact of consciousness, the distinguishing mark of our humanity, gives us, however minimally, a possible opening towards freedom and self-control. Authentic self-knowledge recognises both ends of the dialectic of force: that it treated us like things, and made us into beings who treated others like things. We begin to get some leverage over it when we own the reality of what has been done to *us*, and what, in consequence, we have done to *others*. Only when this acknowledgement has been made are we in a position to start turning ourselves round; only when we know where we are can we begin to plan a way out. When racists, homophobes and women-abusers undergo sensitivity training the expectation is that they will be brought to a recognition of both ends of this cruel paradox: they treated others not as fellow humans, but as objects; but they themselves were formed and manipulated by external forces that worked on them with no regard to their humanity. Only at this moment of recognition can the process of radical transformation, conversion or turning-round, begin.

These processes are hard enough at the individual level; at the group or collective level they are unimaginably more difficult; yet even here astonishing processes of transform-ation are achievable. The Truth and Reconciliation Commission in South Africa was set up to respond to the trauma of the apartheid years. The approach of the commis-sion was based on the apparently monstrous claim that securing acknowledgement, confession and forgiveness were better responses to evil than endless, self-fortifying cycles of revenge. Gobodo-Madikizela is in no doubt:

> The question is no longer *whether* victims can forgive 'evildoers' but whether we – our symbols, language, and politics, our legal, media, and academic institutions – are creating the conditions that encourage alternatives to revenge. We have come to rely too narrowly on retribu-tion as the only legitimate form of justice.[110]

It is here that she makes an interesting and controver-sial point. She wonders if the dynamic between victims and perpetrators has been unduly influenced by narra-tives from the Holocaust experience, which has strongly emphasised remembering rather than dialogue.[111] It may be that the horrifying intensity of the Holocaust made it almost impossible for survivors to take any route other than remembering and holding to account, but subsequent history suggests that if perpetrators and victims are to live on together in the same society, then remembering and recording the horrors that have been perpetrated must be accompanied by dialogue, if healing is to be achieved.

Through dialogue, victims as well as the greater society come to recognise perpetrators as human beings who failed morally, whether through coercion, the perverted convictions of a warped mind, or fear. Far from relieving the pressure on them, recognising the most serious criminals as human intensifies it, because society is thereby able to hold them to greater moral accountability.[112]

Nevertheless, a balancing observation has to be entered here. While South Africa's Truth and Reconciliation Commission has been widely admired, it has also been criticised not for the good it has undoubtedly done, but for the evil it has left unresolved. It may be that the imbalance in its effectiveness is a consequence of the strong Christian influences that prompted it. If the Jewish passion for justice had been added to the Christian passion for reconciliation, a more complete healing of the horrors of the apartheid years might have been achieved. Justice and reconciliation are not opposed to each other, they are antithetic — each balances or completes the other. As Hannah Arendt has shown, declaratory justice is fundamental if the degradation of the victim is to be remedied; but reconciliation is equally fundamental, as Gobodo-Madikizela has shown, if those who have turned against humanity are to be reclaimed by society.

There are hopeful signs that parts of the human community are beginning to understand how the evils of force must be responded to by both justice and reconciliation, if we are to develop healthy communities. In almost every area of conflict on earth there are forgiveness and reconciliation movements at work; and restorative and reformative rather than purely retributive approaches to criminal justice are being tried out. The key thing to remember is Andrea Dworkin's description of the world as 'man–made'. Just as relations between the sexes have traditionally been dominated by male control, so male dominance has characterised many other aspects of the human community, such as religion and politics. To be optimistic for a moment, it is worth remembering that, under the influence of feminist thinkers, men and the institutions they have dominated for centuries have shown themselves capable of repentance and transformation. Most of us have had to negotiate these complexities incompetently, sometimes fearfully. Few of us have the courage of a Martin Luther King or Pius Ncube, compromised saints who swallowed their own fears and stood up to monsters. But we can all do more to lead what Plato called the examined life, the only life he thought worth living. It might have been better to have been brave, but it *is* something to admit we have been cowards rather than to deny it. It might have been finer never to have abused and objectified others, but it *is* something to acknowledge it when we have done so: and it may even be the beginning of radical change in our lives. We need not always allow ourselves to be petrified by force: there are ways we can resist. We are never without hope, and one source of hope is the existence of people who seem to have a capacity for empathy and an indifference to force that is miraculously pure. They are the true saints, who comprise a spiritual singularity in their own right. They are worth thinking about as I bring this book to an end.

We find a clue to the nature of these people in something else written by Simone Weil. In a letter to her parents a couple of weeks before her death in 1943, she discussed the fools in Shakespeare. She said:

> When I saw *Lear* here, I asked myself how it was possible that the unbearably tragic character of these fools had not been obvious long ago to everyone, including myself. There is a class of people in this world . . . and these are the only people who, in fact, are able to tell the truth. All the others lie.[113]

She is saying that only the truly innocent act with unself-conscious truthfulness in all situations. Intriguingly, though he did not use the precise term 'fool', Nietzsche had the same insight when he discussed what he called the psychology of the redeemer. In *The Antichrist* he called Jesus an 'idiot': intended not as an insult, but as a reference to the novels of Dostoevsky. I have found this extract from the art historian John Richardson's *Sacred Monsters, Sacred Masters* helpful in understanding what Nietzsche was getting at. Richardson wrote this about Andy Warhol:

> Andy was born with an innocence and humility that was impregnable – his Slavic spirituality again – and in this respect was a throwback to that Russian phenomenon, the *yurodivyi*: the simpleton whose quasi-divine *naïveté* supposedly protects him against an inimical world. Russian literature's most renowned example is Dostoevsky's Prince Myshkin . . . For all that holy fools are supposedly inviolable, they often turn out to be physically at risk, magnets for aggression . . . True to form, Andy got shot by a demented feminist.[114]

In her biography of Leonard Woolf, Victoria Glendinning
brings another angle to the same phenomenon. Discussing
Woolf's carapace, the protective front he presented to the
world, she said he knew some who were direct, simple
and spiritually unveiled. It made them seem almost like
simpletons; they were 'the sillies' whom Tolstoy thought
'the best people in the world'.[115] Maybe because their
innocence is threatening to the morally compromised
majority, such people are always at risk in our violent
world. The saint seems to be endowed by nature or provi-
dence with an indifference to force in all its forms, and
speaks truth to power at all times and in all places.
Nevertheless, their innocence is unable to protect them
against the impact of force upon their bodies and they
are, in fact, more likely than the rest of us to be its intentional victims. Speaking specifically about Jesus, Weil wrote
that even the man who does not wear the armour of the
lie cannot experience force without being touched by it
to the very soul. While grace can prevent this touch from
corrupting him, it cannot spare him the wound. There is
no escape for any of us from force, from the forms gross
matter assumes in its domination over us, but Jesus
belonged to that tiny group who refuse ever to respect
it. This kind of absolute truthfulness and indifference to
the force that drives the world seems to be an original
endowment of being, not something humans can acquire
by their own effort. When we see it in action, however,
when we encounter the rare person who is totally unimpressed by force in any of its manifestations, we feel
our own cowardice and cravenness coming under judgement. We remember our own shaming compromises with

the bullying pressures of life and, like Peter the Apostle in the courtyard after his betrayal of Jesus, we long to go out and weep bitterly.

There are few of these remarkable people in history, so we should be grateful to Christianity for carrying the memory of one of them through time; but we must also acknowledge that, while there have always been heroic Christians who have followed the way of Jesus, the institution that bears his name has rarely attempted to do so, probably because institutions know intuitively that they are instruments of force. The first rule of institutions is self-preservation, usually at the cost of their original purpose. If the original purpose of Christianity was to carry the spirit of Jesus through history, then it soon fell into the trap of using most of its energies to maintain itself and the life to which it had grown accustomed. While inevitable, this contradiction in Christianity is doubly tragic, because its scripture contains an account of the most complete reversal of the way of force ever dreamt by the human soul. Its most lyrical expression is found in the Sermon on the Mount, where Jesus congratulates his followers for being poor, hungry, bereaved and persecuted. There is irony, even black humour here, but something deeper than irony is present. Jesus takes the measure of all conventional responses to power and the ambiguous gifts it brings and reverses them:

> Ye have heard that it hath been said, An eye for an eye and a tooth for a tooth; but I say unto you, That ye resist not evil: but whosoever shall smite thee on thy right cheek, turn to him the other also . . . Love your enemies,

bless them that curse you, do good to them that hate
you, and pray for them which despitefully use you, and
persecute you.[116]

We see these reversals of the way of force in the crucifixion of Jesus, where he performs in deed what he had
proclaimed in word. He offers no resistance to those who
arrest him. In the midst of the noisy hatred that surrounds
him, he is silent. 'And the chief priests accused him of
many things: but he answered nothing. And Pilate asked
him again, saying, Answerest thou nothing? behold how
many things they witness against thee. But Jesus yet
answered nothing; so that Pilate marvelled.'[117] Jesus refuses
to respect force, either by opposing it or submitting to
it: he ignores it. It is probably not even correct to describe
his response as protest, since that is also a way of noticing
force. No, he disregards its angry presence. If force is the
psychological gravity of the man-made world, we can
only conclude that there was a lightness in Jesus that made
him impervious to what presses other people down. He
seemed impervious to the pressures that bend humans
into shapes of fear or compliance or anger. Thinking about
that, it is strange to contemplate the manner in which his
followers have responded to the weightless indifference
of Jesus to the pressure of force. Hierarchical Christianity
is heavy with the pride of office and the dignity of person;
it is cluttered with ceremonial deference; it is burdened
with brocaded magnificence; it is choreographed with
minute attention to processional precedence; it is ranked
and graded like a hive of bees. Yet, there *he* stands, immense
in his silence. Immense, but not invulnerable. Though

silence magnified him, it could not protect him. Force crushed him and threw him aside.

It is not to be *thought* about, this death-poem of Christ. Nor are we to build theories upon it, though priests have built thousands of them. It is best to let the offence of it stun us into silence. The silence will do its work, if we let it. It does not explain itself. It stands there, a poem made visible. The efficient brutality of the crucifixion distils into a single image the relentless reign of force, the X that turns those who are subjected to it into a thing. And it goes on. It goes on as I write this; as you read it. But something else goes on as well. There are always those, few in any generation, who, having taken the measure of force, know how not to respect it, even if they are crushed in the struggle. Watching them from behind the ramparts of our fear may not give us courage, but it can break our hearts. And that can be a beginning. People like Jesus, who steadfastly refuse to collude with force in any of its forms are inimitable. Their imperviousness to the pressures that manipulate the rest of us seems to be innate, an original virtue. We can be in awe of them, humbled by them, but there is little point in trying to imitate them. Few of us are capable of their complete abnegation of self-protection, but we are all able to live more reflectively and learn to recognise the way evil functions in the human community and try, before it is too late, to atone for its oppressions.

The day after the assassination of Robert Kennedy I took the train from Los Angeles, where he had been shot, to Flagstaff in Arizona. The summer of 1968 was a turbulent and violent episode in American history. The Vietnam

War was at its height and the mood in the country was jagged and angry. Like everyone else that day, I was in a pensive mood as I gazed out of the window of the speeding train. I picked up the book on my lap, Arthur Koestler's *Darkness at Noon*. The epigraph came as a gift that calmed my spirit. It was from Dostoevsky: 'Man, man, one cannot live quite without pity.' If my book has a single message, that is it: though I prefer the stronger word empathy, the ability not only to feel *for* the afflicted, but to feel *with* them. It is the possible remedy for the knowing and unknowing cruelty we do against ourselves and the other creatures with whom we briefly share the earth. One cannot live quite without pity. However, great as that word is, I do not want it to be my last word. My last word has to be *gratitude*, gratitude for being, gratitude for *the fact of a street corner at all*. It shows ingratitude and a lack of imagination to spend the life we've been given stamping, literally or metaphorically, on the lives of others, or sneering contemptuously at how they have chosen to make sense of theirs. It is a harsh world, indescribably cruel. It is a gentle world, unbelievably beautiful. It is a world that can make us bitter, hateful, rabid, destroyers of joy. It is a world that can draw forth tenderness from us, as we lean towards one another over broken gates. It is a world of monsters and saints, a mutilated world, but it is the only one we have been given. We should let it shock us not into hatred or anxiety, but into unconditional love.

NOTES

1: Monster

1. Blake Morrison, *As If*, Granta Books, London 1998, p. 208.
2. Simone Weil, 'The Iliad or the Poem of Force', *Simone Weil: An Anthology*, Grove Press, New York 1986, p. 163.
3. Andrea Dworkin, *Intercourse*, Arrow Books, London 1988.
4. Ibid., p. 31ff.
5. Weil, op. cit., p. 191.
6. Dworkin, op. cit., p. 31ff.
7. Dylan Thomas, 'The Force that Through the Green Fuse Drives the Flower', *The Poems*, J.M. Dent and Sons, London 1974, p. 77.
8. Arthur Schopenhauer, *The World as Will and Representation*, Dover Publications, New York 1966, vol. 2, p. 556.
9. Weil, op. cit., pp. 184–5.
10. Pumla Gobodo-Madikizela, *A Human Being Died that Night*, Portobello Books, London 2006, p. 46.
11. J. Gilligan, *Violence: Our Deadly Epidemic and Its Causes*, G.P. Putnam, New York 1996, p. 106.
12. Philip Zimbardo, *The Lucifer Effect*, Rider, London 2007, p. 5.
13. Ibid, p. x.
14. Friedrich Nietzsche, *On the Genealogy of Morals*, II.6, in *The Basic Writings of Nietzsche*, ed. Walter Kaufmann, The Modern Library, New York 1992, p. 501.
15. Michel Foucault, *Discipline and Punish: The Birth of the Prison*, translated from the French by Alan Sheridan, Vintage Books, New York 1995, p. 1ff.
16. Zimbardo, op. cit., p. 281.
17. Quoted in John Gray, *Black Mass*, Allen Lane, London 2007, p. 167.
18. Julia Layton, 'What Is Waterboarding?' October 31 2006, at http://people.howstuffworks.com/water-boarding.htm.

19. Gray, op. cit., p. 158.
20. Quoted from the report in Zimbardo, op. cit., p. 403.
21. Quoted in Diana Athill, *Stet*, Granta, London 2000, pp. 70–71.
22. Athill, op. cit., p. 75.
23. Hannah Arendt, 'Eichmann in Jerusalem', in *The Portable Hannah Arendt*, Penguin, London 2000, p. 379.
24. Gitta Sereny, *Albert Speer,* Macmillan 1995, p. 719.
25. Weil, op. cit., p. 192.
26. Arendt, op. cit., pp. 378–9.
27. Gobodo-Madikizela, op. cit., pp. 98–9.
28. Arendt, op. cit., p. 375.

2: Pity

29. Victoria Glendinning, *Leonard Woolf*, Simon and Schuster, London 2006, p. 31.
30. 'At the Burial of the Dead' in *The Scottish Book of Common Prayer*, Cambridge University Press, Edinburgh 1929.
31. Paul's First Letter to the Corinthians, 15.26.
32. Loren Eiseley, *The Immense Journey,* Vintage Books, New York 1959, p. 173ff.
33. Letter to J.D. Hooker, 13th July, 1856, Darwin Archives, Cambridge University Library.
34. Benedict Allen, *Into the Abyss*, Faber and Faber, London 2006, p. 252.
35. John Berger, *About Looking,* Vintage Books, New York 1991, p. 7.
36. Berger, op. cit., p. 3.
37. Danielle Nierenberg, 'Factory Farming in the Developing World', http://www.worldwatch.org/pubs/mag/2003/163 (published in *Worldwatch Magazine*, May/June 2003, Vol. 16, No. 3).
38. Robert Crawford, 'The Bad Shepherd' in *Selected Poems*, Jonathan Cape, London 2005, p. 99.
39. Claudia Tarry, 'Stuffed! The Terrible Truth about Turkeys', http://www.viva.org.uk/campaigns/turkeys/turkeys-companyinfo.htm.
40. Genesis 1.26.

41. Robert Pogue Harrison, *The Dominion of the Dead*, University of Chicago Press, Chicago 2003, p. 8.
42. Genesis 3.1.
43. Genesis 1.29.
44. Genesis 6.5–6.
45. Friedrich Nietzsche, *The Birth of Tragedy*, Penguin Classics, London 1993, p. 53.
46. Genesis 1.3 4.
47. Genesis 1.26–27.
48. Robert Hughes, *Things I Didn't Know*, Harvill Secker, London 2006, p. 291.

3: Soul

49. William Shakespeare, *King Lear*, V. iii 323.
50. Harrison, op. cit., p. 136.
51. Ibid., p. 137.
52. Dante's *Inferno*, 3.55–7.
53. Ibid., pp. *xi*, 21.
54. Robert Alter, *The Five Books of Moses*, Norton, New York and London 2004, p. 21.
55. Virginia Woolf, *The Waves*, Penguin Classics, London 2000, pp. 114–15.
56. 'At the Burial of the Dead' in *The Scottish Book of Common Prayer*, Cambridge University Press, Edinburgh 1929, p. 458.
57. Sigmund Freud, *Beyond the Pleasure Principle and Other Writings*, Penguin Books, London 2003, p. 78.
58. Matthew 10.28.
59. Friedrich Nietzsche, *Human, All Too Human [5]*, in *The Portable Nietzsche*, tr. Walter Kaufmann, Penguin Books, London 1976, p. 52.
60. Isaiah 38.18.
61. I Corinthians 15.35–8; 42–4.
62. William Shakespeare, *Hamlet*, III. iii. 76–98.
63. Robert Funk and Roy Hoover, *The Five Gospels*, Scribner, New York 1993, p. 361.
64. Luke 18.25.
65. Luke 16.19–26.
66. The Quran, tr. J.M. Rodwell, Everyman's Library, J.M. Dent,

London 1909, VII. 40–1, 50: pp. 297–8; LVI. 41–4, 51–2: p. 66; XXXVII. 43–6: p. 81; XLIV. 43–53: p. 90; LVI. 15–24: p. 67.

67. Berger, op. cit., pp. 11 and 13.

4: Suffering

68. Auden, 'Musée des Beaux Arts', in *Collected Poems*, Faber and Faber, London 1976, p. 146.
69. W.H. Auden, 'Funeral Blues', ibid., p. 120.
70. Bishop Butler to John Wesley in John Wesley, *Works*, xiii, p. 449.
71. Job 40.2.
72. Ryszard Kapuściński, *Travels with Herodotus*, Allen Lane, London 2007, p. 226.
73. Friedrich Nietzsche, *The Gay Science*, tr. Walter Kaufmann, Vintage Books, New York 1974, p. 182.
74. Richard Rorty, *Philosophy and Social Hope*, Penguin, London 1999, p. 208.
75. Stephen Vincent Benét, *John Brown's Body*, Rinehart and Company, New York 1928, p. 336.

5: Comedy

76. W.H. Auden, 'In Memory of W.B. Yeats' in *Collected Poems*, Faber and Faber, London 1976, p. 197.
77. Daniel Albright, notes on Yeats in W.B. Yeats, *The Poems,* ed. Daniel Albright, Everyman's Library, London 1990, p. 844.
78. Yeats, 'Crazy Jane Talks with the Bishop', op. cit., p. 309.
79. Lewis Hyde, *The Gift: Imagination and the Erotic Life of Property*, Vintage Books, New York 1983, p. 193.
80. Mark 15.31.
81. Tennessee Williams, *Cat on a Hot Tin Roof and Other Plays*, Penguin, London 1976, p. 7.
82. Ibid., pp. 317–18.
83. Ibid., p. 308.
84. Ibid., p. 304.
85. Margaret Drabble, a review of *The Power of Delight* by John Bayley, *New Statesman*, 16th May, 2005.
86. A.E. Housman, IX from *Last Poems* in *Poetry and Prose: A Selection*, Hutchinson Educational, London 1972, p. 117.

87. Alan Hollinghurst, *The Line of Beauty*, Picador, London 2004, p. 500.
88. Luke 22.61–2.
89. George Mackay Brown, 'Song for St Andrew's Day' in *The Collected Poems*, John Murray, London 2005, p. 387.
90. John 21.15–17.
91. Percy Bysshe Shelley, in *The New Oxford Book of English Verse, 1250–1950*, ed. Helen Gardner, Clarendon Press, Oxford 1972, p. 580.
92. Cyril Connolly, *The Unquiet Grave*, Hamish Hamilton, London 1945, p. 25.
93. Iris Murdoch, *The Sovereignty of Good*, Arc, London 1985, p. 59.
94. Marcel Proust, *The Captive*, tr. C.K. Scott Moncrieff, Chatto and Windus, London 1960, vol. 1, pp. 249–50. The version quoted is translated by Richard Davenport-Hines, in *A Night at the Majestic*, Faber and Faber, London 2006, p. 310.
95. Kurtz's last words to Marlow in Joseph Conrad's *Heart of Darkness*.
96. Iain Crichton Smith, 'She Teaches Lear' and 'Old Woman' in *Selected Poems*, Carcanet Press, Manchester 1985, pp. 52 and 18.
97. Joseph Meeker, *The Comedy of Survival: Literary Ecology and a Play Ethic*, University of Arizona Press, Tucson 1997, p. 20.
98. Richard Mabey, *Nature Cure*, Pimlico, London 2006, p. 199.

6: Saint

99. Osip Mandelstam, 'Stalin Epigram' in Nadezhda Mandelstam, *Hope Against Hope*, tr. Max Hayward, Collins Harvill, London 1989, p.13.
100. Dworkin, op. cit., p. 48.
101. Ibid., p. 51.
102. Ibid., p. 53ff.
103. Ibid., 42.
104. Ibid., pp. 43 and 47.
105. Immanuel Kant in 'The Philosophy of Kant: Immanuel Kant Moral and Political Writings' in *Foundations of the Metaphysics of Morals*, ed. Carl Friedrich, The Modern Library, New York 1993, p. 200.

106. See Taylor Branch, *Parting of the Waters*, Simon and Schuster, New York 1988 and Morton Halperin, Jerry Berman, Robert Borosage and Christine Marwick, *The Lawless State*, Penguin Books, New York 1976.

107. Dworkin, op. cit., p. 189.

108. Loc. cit.

109. Virginia Woolf, *A Room of One's Own*, Penguin Classics, London 2000, p. 31.

110. Gobodo-Madikizela, op. cit., p. 118.

111. Ibid., p. 119.

112. Loc. cit.

113. Weil, op. cit., pp. 1–2.

114. John Richardson, *Sacred Monsters, Sacred Masters*, Pimlico, London 2002, p. 257.

115. Victoria Glendinning, *Leonard Woolf*, Simon and Schuster, London 2006, p. 36.

116. Matthew 5.38, 39, 44.

117. Mark 15.3–5.

PERMISSIONS

Various publishers and Estates have generously given permission to use extracts from the following copyright works:

Michel Foucault, *Discipline and Punish: The Birth of the Prison*, translated by Alan Sheridan, first published as *Surveiller et punir: Naissance de la prison* by Editions Gallimard 1975, Allen Lane 1975, copyright Alan Sheridan, 1977

Eleanor Wilner, 'Reading the Bible Backwards' from *Reversing the Spell: New and Selected Poems*, Copper Canyon Press, Port Townsend, 1997

W.H. Auden, 'Musée des Beaux-Arts', from *Collected Poems*, Faber, London, 1976

W.B. Yeats, 'Crazy Jane Talks to the Bishop', reproduced by permission of A.P. Watt on behalf of Gráinne Yeats

The Authorised King James Version of the Bible, reproduced by permission of the Lord Advocate's Office and the Scottish Bible Board

BIBLIOGRAPHY

Allen, Benedict, *Into the Abyss*, Faber and Faber, London, 2006

Alter, Robert, *The Five Books of Moses*, Norton, New York and London, 2004

Arendt, Hannah, *Eichmann in Jerusalem: A Report on the Banality of Evil*, Penguin, London, 1963

Athill, Diana, *Stet*, Granta, London, 2000

Auden, W.H., *Collected Poems*, Faber and Faber, London, 1976

Benét, Stephen Vincent, *John Brown's Body*, Doubleday, Doran & Co., New York, 1928

Berger, John, *About Looking*, Vintage Books, New York, 1991

Branch, Taylor, *Parting of the Waters*, Simon and Schuster, New York, 1988

Brown, George Mackay, *The Collected Poems*, John Murray, London, 2005

Connolly, Cyril, *The Unquiet Grave*, Hamish Hamilton Library, London, 1945

Crawford, Robert, *Selected Poems*, Jonathan Cape, London, 2005

Darwin, Charles, letter to J.D. Hooker, 13th July, 1856, Darwin Archives, Cambridge University Library

Davenport-Hines, Richard, *A Night at the Majestic*, Faber and Faber, London, 2006

Diski, Jenny, *After These Things*, Little, Brown, London, 2004

Dworkin, Andrea, *Intercourse*, Arrow Books, London, 1988

Eiseley, Loren, *The Immense Journey*, Vintage Books, New York, 1959

Foucault, Michel, *Discipline and Punish: The Birth of the Prison*, translated from the French by Alan Sheridan, Vintage Books, New York, 1995

Freud, Sigmund, *Beyond the Pleasure Principle and Other Writings*, Penguin Books, London, 2003

Funk, Robert and Hoover, Roy, *The Five Gospels*, Scribner, New York, 1993

Gilligan, J., *Violence: Our Deadly Epidemic and its Causes*, G.P. Putnam, New York, 1996

Glendinning, Victoria, *Leonard Woolf*, Simon and Schuster, London, 2006

Gobodo-Madikizela, Pumla, *A Human Being Died that Night*, Portobello Books, London, 2006

Gray, John, *Black Mass*, Allen Lane, London, 2007

Halperin, Morton, Jerry Berman, Robert Borosage, Christine Marwick, *The Lawless State*, Penguin Books, New York, 1976

Harrison, Robert Pogue, *The Dominion of the Dead*, University of Chicago Press, Chicago, 2003

Hollinghurst, Alan, *The Line of Beauty*, Picador, London, 2004

Houseman, A.E., *Last Poems in Poetry and Prose: A Selection*, Hutchinson Educational, London, 1972

Hughes, Robert, *Things I Didn't Know*, Harvill Secker, London, 2006

Hyde, Lewis, *The Gift: How the Creative Spirit Transforms the World*, Canongate Books, Edinburgh, 2006

Kant, Immanuel, *The Philosophy of Kant: Immanuel Kant Moral and Political Writings*, ed. Carl Friedrich, The Modern Library, New York, 1993

Kapuściński, Ryszard, *Travels with Herodotus*, Allan Lane, London, 2007

Layton, Julia, 'What is Waterboarding?' October 31, 2006 at http://people.howstuffworks.com/water-boarding.htm

Mabey, Richard, *Nature Cure*, Pimlico, London, 2006

Mandelstam, Nadezhda, *Hope Against Hope*, translated by Max Hayward, Collins Harvill, London, 1989

Meeker, Joseph, *The Comedy of Survival: Literary Ecology and a Play Ethic*, University of Arizona Press, Tucson, 1997

Morrison, Blake, *As If*, Granta Books, London, 1998

Murdoch, Iris, *The Sovereignty of Good*, Arc, London, 1985

Nierenberg, Danielle, 'Stuffed! The Terrible Truth about Turkeys', http://www.viva.org.uk/campaigns/turkeys/turkeys-companyinfo.htm; 'Factory Farming in the Developing World', http://www.worldwatch.org/pubs/mag/2003/163, *World Watch Magazine*, May/June, 2003

Nietzsche, Friedrich, *On the Genealogy of Morals. The Basic*

Writings of Neitzsche, ed. Walter Kaufmann, The Modern Library, New York, 1992

Nietzsche, Friedrich, *The Birth of Tragedy*, Penguin Classics, London, 1993

Nietzsche, Friedrich, *Human, All Too Human: A Book for Free Spirits.* In *The Portable Nietzsche,* selected and translated by Walter Kaufmann, Penguin Books, London, 1976

Nietzsche, Friedrich, *The Gay Science*, translated by Walter Kaufmann, Vintage Books, New York, 1974

Proust, Marcel, *The Captive*, Vol. 1,. Chatto and Windus, London, 1960

Qur'an, The, translated by J. M. Rodwell, Everyman's Library, J. M. Dent, London, 1909

Richardson, John, *Sacred Monsters, Sacred Masters*, Pimlico, London, 2002

Rorty, Richard, *Philosophy and Social Hope*, Penguin, London, 1999

Schopenhauer, Arthur, *The World as Will and Representation*, Vol. 2, Dover Publications, New York, 1966

The Scottish Book of Common Prayer, Cambridge University Press, Edinburgh, 1929

Shelley, Percy Bysshe, in *The New Oxford Book of English Verse, 1250–1950*, ed. Gardener, Helen.

Smith, Iain Crichton, *Selected Poems*, Carcanet Press, Manchester, 1985

Sereny, Gitta, *Albert Speer,* Macmillan, 1995

Tarry, Claudia, 'Stuffed! The Terrible Truth about Turkeys', http://www.viva.org.uk/campaigns/turkeys/turkeys-companyinfo.htm

Thomas, Dylan, *The Poems*, J.M. Dent and Sons, London 1974

Weil, Simone, *An Anthology.* Grove Press, New York, 1986

Williams, Tennessee, *Cat on a Hot Tin Roof and Other Plays*, Penguin, London, 1976

Woolf, Virginia, *The Waves*, Penguin Classics, London, 2000

Woolf, Virginia, *A Room of One's Own*, Penguin Classics, London, 2000

Yeats, W. B., *The Poems*, ed. Daniel Albright, Everyman's Library, London, 1992

Zimbardo, Philip, *The Lucifer Effect*, Rider, London, 2007

INDEX